# WOMEN OF FAIR HOPE

# WOMEN OF
# FAIR HOPE

PAUL M. GASTON

*MERCER UNIVERSITY*
*LAMAR MEMORIAL LECTURES*
*No. 25*

THE UNIVERSITY OF GEORGIA PRESS
ATHENS

© 1984 by the University of Georgia Press
Athens, Georgia 30602

All rights reserved

Set in 11 on 13 pt. Linotron 202 Baskerville

The paper in this book meets the guidelines for
permanence and durability of the Committee on
Production Guidelines for Book Longevity of the
Council on Library Resources.

Printed in the United States of America

88  87  86          5  4  3  2

Library of Congress Cataloging in Publication Data

Gaston, Paul M.
Women of Fair Hope.

(Mercer University Lamar memorial lectures; no. 25)
Bibliography: p.
Includes index.
1. Women—Alabama—Fairhope—Biography—
Addresses, essays, lectures. 2. Social reformers—
Alabama—Fairhope—History—Addresses, essays,
lectures. 3. Utopias. 4. Single tax. I. Title.
II. Series: Lamar memorial lectures; no. 25.
HQ1412.G37    1984      305.4'09761'21      84-103
ISBN 0-8203-0718-1
ISBN 0-8203-0840-4 (pbk.)

*For*
*Margaret Chinta Gaston*
*and the memory of her grandmother*
*Margaret Nichols Gaston*

# Contents

# Foreword

DURING THE DEPRESSION OF THE 1890S AND AMID THE reform ferment of that decade, Ernest B. Gaston, a young Iowa newspaperman indignant over the excesses of Gilded Age industrialism, led a group of midwesterners to the eastern shore of Mobile Bay where they established the communitarian settlement of Fairhope. There in south Alabama these colonists attempted to put into practice Henry George's theory of the single tax.

In *Progress and Poverty* (1879), George, a self-educated eonomist, had observed that the rapid progress being made by the American economy had failed to alleviate the poverty in which many Americans lived. He believed that this paradox existed because a few individuals were profiting from the rental of land and from the increase in land values generated by the community— an increase that landowners had not earned. Rather than tax the output of capital and labor, government, George argued, should tax only this unearned increment on land. Because the community created land values, the community should benefit from them. The single tax, he contended, would meet the costs of government and would render other taxes unnecessary. The theory was endorsed by people throughout the world.

At Fairhope, Gaston and his followers established a system of "cooperative individualism" wherein virtually

all property except land was privately owned. The community made decisions regarding the raising and
spending of revenues derived from land rents; private
enterprise ran most other facets of the economy. Such
an arrangement, the Fairhopers believed, would encourage individual initiative and at the same time promote the general welfare.

Unusual in its economic base, Fairhope departed from
convention in other respects as well, notably in the expanded opportunity for self-fulfillment and community
service afforded to women. In one way or another, three
remarkable women were associated with the Fairhope
experiment: Nancy Lewis, who wanted more from life
than a nominal freedom; Marie Howland, who spent a
lifetime crusading for the good society; and Marietta
Johnson, who made her mark as an innovative, inspiring
educator. If only two of these women were Fairhopers
proper, all were indeed "women of fair hope."

Paul M. Gaston is peculiarly suited to have delivered
the lectures—the first in the Lamar series to deal specifically with women—that provide the basis for this book.
Himself a native of Fairhope, a lineal descendant of the
men who led the colony for eighty years, and a scholar
of high attainment, Professor Gaston brings to his subject the knowledge and passion of the participant and
the craft of the historian. His audiences at Mercer University displayed an avid curiosity about Fairhope and a
keen appreciation of his skill as a lecturer. We at Mercer
thank him for this fascinating contribution to the study
of the South that so very ably fulfills the purpose of the
Lamar Memorial Lectures.

Wayne Mixon
for the
Lamar Memorial Lectures Committee

# *Preface*

THE INVITATION TO DELIVER THE TWENTY-FIFTH ANNUAL Lamar Memorial Lectures came shortly after I decided to write a history of the Fairhope Single Tax Colony, the Yankee enclave in the Deep South where I had grown up. I knew the Fairhope story would be absorbing and instructive, but it did not seem to me to be particularly southern. Uncertain about a subject for the Lamar Lectures—a series devoted to southern history, culture, and literature—I nonetheless accepted the invitation because a southern historian must feel both pride and a sense of obligation on being asked to become part of such a distinguished tradition. Unwilling to take time away from my Fairhope work, however, I wavered until my daughter remonstrated with me to choose an aspect of it for my topic. Thus admonished and guided, I fixed on the careers of Nancy Lewis, Marie Howland, and Marietta Johnson, remarkable women of hope, each of whom pursued her special vision of a world both freer and happier. An account of their personal journeys and of the ways those journeys shaped and were shaped by the Fairhope colony offered intriguing possibilities. Once into the subject I was relieved to hear the echo of familiar southern-history themes. I was also pleased that my topic became the first in the lecture series to focus on the lives of southern women.

I want to thank Professor Henry Y. Warnock of the Mercer University History Department for inviting me to give the lectures and, along with his wife, for seeing that my stay in Macon was full of enjoyment and good fellowship. Nancy Anderson's introduction was a special pleasure, as was the splendid gathering at Fran and Wayne Mixon's. The lively interest in the Fairhope experiment and the three women who were part of it that I found both in the lecture hall and in less formal surroundings was especially gratifying.

I am grateful to Charles East, formerly of the University of Georgia Press, both for his gentle prodding to get the manuscript to him and for his personal interest in the Fairhope story. The first chapter is virtually unchanged from the lecture, but the other two are considerably longer. I am obliged to Mr. East for letting me expand them. I am indebted to the University of Georgia Press and to the Lamar Memorial Lectures Committee for permitting me to publish the Nancy Lewis essay in the Summer 1984 issue of the *Virginia Quarterly Review*.

For such a small book I have received a disproportionate amount of aid and good counsel. Four research assistants—Ann-Marie Bolton, Todd Cooper, Lisa Fishbeck, and Chris Lee—helped with careful and tedious work and a generous interest in the women. Rebecca Penrose lent a hand from London, and Donna Evleth did her best to track down Marie Howland materials in France. With an assist from Lottie McCauley and her associates at the Corcoran Department of History, Kathleen Miller saw the manuscript through the word processor and cheerfully made every alteration I was lured into by this new technological wonder.

Many persons shared their materials and findings with me, and guided me to obscure sources. I am especially grateful to Pierce E. Frederick, Ray P. Reynolds, Robert Offergeld, Dolores Hayden, Renie Carlson, Phyllis Lobdell, Jere R. Daniell, Robert H. Leavitt, Jasper S. Hunt, and the late C. F. W. Coker. Librarians at Columbia University, the University of Kansas, Emporia State University, the California State University at Fresno, and the Fairhope Public Library responded to inquiries, sent copies of letters, or made available collections I needed. Directors of the School of Organic Education in Fairhope gave me the use of the school's incomplete but invaluable archives. The Fairhope Single Tax Colony archives, extensive and well preserved, were always open to me and I thank especially Mary Gaston Godard and Gale W. Rowe for their cooperation, assistance, and encouragement.

The manuscript has been read by many friends and colleagues and is much the better for their suggestions. Edward L. Ayers, David Levin, Rosetta Lewis, C. Stuart McGehee, Roger Shattuck, and Burton Spivak read the Nancy Lewis chapter. Marjorie Spruill Wheeler and Janet Letts read the chapters on Nancy Lewis and Marie Howland. Jeanne Pietig read the Marietta Johnson chapter, as did several Fairhope friends who knew Mrs. Johnson well: Joyce Totten Bishop, Dorothy Beiser Cain, Helen Porter Dyson, Sam Dyson, Claire Totten Gray, Eleanor Coutant Nichols, and Marvin Nichols. One version or another of the entire manuscript was read by William W. Abbot, Robert D. Cross, Chinta Gaston, Mary Gaston, Jacquelyn Dowd Hall, Lynda Morgan, Marcia Borst Klenbort, and Elizabeth Macdonald Wilkinson. I am deeply grateful to all of these readers for their concern and support as well as for the improvements they helped me to make.

I revised the manuscript for publication during a semester when I was freed from teaching by a grant from the Rockefeller Foundation.

My father, the late C. A. Gaston, celebrated his ninetieth birthday shortly after I gave the lectures. He knew all three women, told me things about them I could have learned from no other source, and, as always, was a wise and supportive counselor. I shall miss him.

PAUL M. GASTON

Charlottesville, Virginia
October 29, 1983

ONE

# The Discovery of Nancy Lewis

I was born and reared in Fairhope, Alabama, a "utopian" community, a single-tax colony founded on the eastern shore of Mobile Bay in 1894, but until a few years ago I had never heard of Nancy Lewis. I might never have learned about her if I had not decided to write a book about the town's history. In such a book, I knew, women would occupy a special place. I knew this because my memories of growing up were rich with examples of strong women who influenced my values and aspirations as they helped to shape the history of the community. Research in the colony archives strengthened and expanded these impressions. I learned, for example, that the Fairhope plan for justice and equal rights emerged from the same ferment that spawned new movements in the late nineteenth century for women's liberation—movements which shared with the Fairhope plan many assumptions and goals. I learned, too, that the new colony immediately attracted independent, talented women who established a flourishing sisterhood, participated in the governance of the community, and stamped the experiment with their hopes and insights.

Marie Howland and Marietta Johnson, two of the three principals in these lectures, stand out as two of Fairhope's most illustrious figures. Both were well known to me before I started my work. I also knew something about most of the other pioneer women, including many who had died before I was born. But I had never heard of Nancy Lewis. It seemed ironic, then, that she should be the first Fairhope woman my research in the colony archives led me to. Before long, caught up in more ironies, I was obsessed with a need to discover everything I could about her and to learn what she had discovered about Fairhope.

An enigmatic entry in the minutes book of the Fairhope Industrial Association introduced me to her. The date was January 22, 1895. Negotiations were under way for the purchase of a two-hundred-acre parcel of land, the second acquisition since the arrival of the colonists two months earlier. The minutes betrayed concern over a claim one Nancy Lewis was apparently making to part of the desired tract. Later, in the February 2 entry, I found out more about her and about the delicate negotiations. She and some of her family were, in fact, living on land which was said to belong to the estate of a John Bowen. Now, however, she was retreating from her previous position, admitting that the Bowen estate, not she, had the title to the land. She also was reconsidering her previous refusal to sell out and move and was reported to be "favorably inclined" toward the idea. The February 7 minutes report a successful outcome for the association: Nancy Lewis agreed to "surrender all her claims" to the land and, for $100, to sell to the association all her improvements on it.[1]

With this impediment removed, the secretary reported the "purchase of 200 acres of Bowen land including 40 acres claimed by Nancy Lewis . . . for $250.00." A later entry tells of a written contract sealing the Lewis agreement. I searched through the colony's file drawer of deeds to find this document—charred by a 1951 office fire, but still legible—bearing Nancy Lewis's well-formed signature. Here the improvements—"houses, sheds, fences, orchards, clearings"—are enumerated and the owner is given sixty days to move. The records do not tell us when she left, but the March 9 minutes report that one of the association officers was preparing to move into her old home.[2]

My first reading of this episode made me wonder why some arrangement had not been made to take Nancy Lewis into the association. Why, I wondered, had it been necessary to buy her out? If, indeed, she had been "squatting" on land legally purchased by the colony, why not swap an association membership for the release of her potentially troublesome claim? In this way one hundred scarce dollars would have been saved, the title to the land made secure, another member added to the tiny band of colonists, and Nancy Lewis might have gone on living where she was, on land cleared and fenced, in a familiar and comfortable home surrounded by vineyards and fruit trees.

What seemed especially incongruous was the hint that the very act of acquiring land to demonstrate the Fairhope plan—a plan above all else to free the land from monopolists and speculators and reserve it for honest users—trapped the Fairhopers in a compromise of principle. Surely it was not meant to work that way; how could it be when the idealists who had brought their few possessions and their many dreams with them from Iowa, Ohio, Minnesota, Pennsylvania, and Canada were driven by an acute sense of the injustices under which men and women lived and a corresponding confidence in the power of their plan to right social wrongs?

My grandfather, Ernest B. Gaston, had led the founding party to Baldwin County where they were now start-

ing up their experiment. He had been the chief architect of the Fairhope constitution, and for the next four
decades he would be the community's unrivaled leader
and spokesman.[3] He died a month before my tenth
birthday (I was the youngest of his eleven grandchildren), but I can never remember when I did not have
an enormous respect for his integrity and his passion
for justice. I needed, then, to review the principles on
which the experiment was formed and then to see how
they could accommodate the troubling tale of Nancy
Lewis and her lost land.

The Fairhope idea emerged from the suffering and creative ferment of the late nineteenth century, and the
founding of the colony in 1894 was one statement of
how Americans might simultaneously harness the
power and subdue the cruelty of industrial capitalism.
In my grandfather's writings from this time I found
powerful indictments of social wrongs—he wrote of the
"enormous waste of human energy and natural resources" and of the "hideous injustice and cruelty" of
rampant individualism and unrestrained competition—
along with insistence that good theories, properly applied, offered a way out. In the history of reform, he
believed, "those who make good theories work and
prove the value of proposed social solutions by practical
demonstration will do far more to move the world than
the wisest and most brilliant theorists."[4]

The search for the right "good theory" on which to
base a practical demonstration began soon after he was
graduated from Drake University, in his hometown of
Des Moines, Iowa, in 1886; it was completed by early
1894, when he drafted a plan for a model colony which

was to be called Fairhope. Out of the swirl of reform thought and experiments he gradually crystallized a unique scheme to realize his vision of a society in which free men and women would cooperate for the common welfare while they perfected their own skills and followed their own interests. When he began his quest he was especially impressed by the writings of Edward Bellamy, Laurence Gronlund, and other socialist authors. He also followed closely the history of the many cooperative colonies that were founded in these years, and in 1890 he made an unsuccessful attempt to establish one of his own.[5] This was followed by two years of intellectually enriching but politically barren work for the Populist party in Iowa.

Returning in late 1893 to the idea of a cooperative colony, my grandfather was guided increasingly by the writings of Henry George, whose ideas inspired him to work out his own blend of cooperation and individualism. His doctrine, "cooperative individualism," identified land as the key element in the problem of social organization. By now Grandfather was concluding that most of the cooperative colonies, too rigidly bound to socialist theories, hemmed individuals in and warped community growth because they required too much central direction to determine what should be produced, by whom, and for what wages. In practice these cooperative efforts were no antidote to the common enemy of unbridled individualism, but only a recipe for frustration and failure. George believed that poverty amidst plenty and exploitation of free people in a democratic country stemmed from the monopoly of natural resources, from the private ownership of land. This theory seemed to offer a way out. According to George, there was no need for government to direct the behavior and confiscate the earnings of labor and capital if all people had equal access to the land, the common heritage of mankind. *"We must make land common property,"* he proclaimed.[6] All else—or nearly all else—could safely be left to the individual.

To make a workable demonstration of this idea, Grandfather planned a colony in which all land would belong to the association. Members would pay into the common treasury an annual rental, based on the value of the land they leased, thus simulating the single tax on land values favored by George. It was in this way, Grandfather believed, that community-created values— that is, land values—would be returned to the whole community, while privately created values, the returns on labor and capital, would remain with the individual. Grandfather was too much of a cooperationist to think of anything but community ownership and management of public utilities ("natural monopolies," he called them), and he had other cooperative ideas as well. He was strong for a community-owned merchandising store, and he believed that communal decisions concerning the setting and spending of land rents, along with full democracy in colony government, would result in cooperative ventures and attitudes, all free from coercion of any sort.

Such was the theory and the plan. How, then, had it happened that the Fairhopers, in almost their first major communal decision, had wrenched Nancy Lewis's homestead from her? Puzzling over the matter, but meanwhile carrying on with other research, I happened one day to ask my father, who was three years old when he arrived with the founding party and who would succeed his father as colony secretary forty-one years later, if he had ever heard of a Nancy Lewis. "Oh yes," he replied. "She was the colored woman who was living on the land the colonists bought."[7]

That answer, of course, opened up questions that had not been asked. As a southern historian I should have been alert to them all along because nothing happens in the South without race soon becoming a crucial issue—testing, defining, and illuminating values and assumptions and shaping public policies. Now I had to ask what race was to mean to these northern reformers—these men and women who had grown up faithful to the party of Lincoln, the Emancipator—as they fashioned their utopia in the Deep South. Before he left Iowa my grandfather wrote that "*use* gives the only right to control of land," and he thundered out his belief that legal titles to land were "no more evidence of *moral right* than the bills of sale in which the unfortunate blacks were held in bondage but a few years since in our land."[8] Nancy Lewis could hardly have said it better: human slavery and private ownership of land were moral equivalents, both abhorrent. In this first encounter, however, local custom easily overrode abstract principle and Nancy Lewis was displaced.

Three years after this episode my grandfather wrote candidly and extensively about the intimate relationship between race and reform. The occasion was an editorial response to the criticism of a disillusioned potential supporter who had decided to give up on the Fairhopers because, as he put it, they "altogether refuse the entry of colored people on the same terms as others." There was no evasion in the reply: "The criticism of our friend," Grandfather stated, "illustrates anew the difficulties and differences of opinion arising in the effort to determine how far we can practically go in the 'application of correct theories' within a general condition of applied in-

correct ones, over which we have no control." Racial
discrimination—especially when it thwarted access to
the land—was wrong, he wrote. "We believe," he went
on to proclaim, "in 'universal equality'—equality of
rights"; no man had "more moral or natural right to any
particular portion of the earth, the common heritage of
mankind, than any other of his fellow men." This being
so, the question was clear: should the Fairhope Association "follow the naked principle of equality unreserv-
edly, regardless of conditions existing?" He could not
recommend it, he concluded, for to do so would likely
mean destruction of the colony.[9]

Thus, to preserve the experiment he agreed that it
must be for whites only. At the same time he made it
clear that the "whites only" policy was a fundamental
contradiction of the "good theory" on which the Fairhope practical demonstration was based. The compromise was perhaps made easier by the belief that, at
bottom, racial prejudice was a function of economic injustice and that, insofar as the Fairhope demonstration
might help to point the way to a better economic order,
it was hastening the day when racism might disappear.
Manifestations of racial prejudice, Grandfather wrote
after the Springfield, Illinois, race riot in 1908, "will
continue and will increase in bitterness as industrial conditions get more severe. They constitute one of the most
serious menaces of the future. The only remedy is economic freedom."[10] On other occasions he stressed the
common predicament of whites and blacks. Southern
sharecropping, for example, ensnared both races in a
new form of slavery so that "the obligation yet owing to
the negro and the white is to throw open to all the
natural resources from which all human wants are supplied by labor."[11] Closer to home, always alert to the
possibilities of practical demonstration, he wrote of

starting up a single-tax colony in the black community adjacent to Fairhope: "It would be an excellent thing for them and us," he wrote, "as well as greatly enlarge the possible magnitude of our demonstration of the advantage of the single tax."[12]

No such colony ever got beyond the talking stage. Nor did economic conditions in the country at large promise to mitigate the force of racial prejudice. In these circumstances, given their considered segregation policy, about all that was left to concerned Fairhopers was to speak out against racist excesses and, within the limits of their power and vision, hold to standards of decency and fair play. Thus, Grandfather did such things as oppose the calling of a state constitutional convention because he believed, quite correctly, that its main purpose was to disfranchise blacks. "We shall certainly vote against it," he warned, "and advise everyone else to do likewise."[13] Lynchings brought outrage to his newspaper; they were "never excusable," he wrote, and their frequency "shows how thin is the veneer of civilization."[14] When it appeared in Fairhope in the 1920s, he attacked and ridiculed the Ku Klux Klan. Lecturing the Town Council on the "Invisible Empire," he said that the "creator had not endowed men . . . with invisibility," and he told them he could see nothing American in an Empire, "invisible or otherwise."[15]

Meanwhile, what of Nancy Lewis? Her exclusion from colony land is a poignant symbol of the ways in which racial values and customs have baffled and constrained even the most sincere reformers. But I don't want to make this an essay on race and reform in Fairhope, interesting though that subject would be to pursue.

From the beginning, from the first time I read her
name in the minutes book, I developed an insatiable
curiosity about her as a person. For one thing, it was
easy for me to imagine where she lived for I had played
on the very spot many times as a boy. Why, I wondered,
had she come to that place? Who was she? What were
her feelings about the land? Was there something she
was searching for? Was there some intangible bond link-
ing her search to the mission that had brought my
grandfather to the identical plot of ground, to dispute
its occupancy with her? How was I to find answers to
these questions?

My search began with the federal census. The 1900
data told me that Nancy Lewis was then a fifty-seven-
year-old widow who had had twelve children, only five of
whom were still living. As I was to learn later, she was
fifty-nine, not fifty-seven, and she had had six children,
not twelve—errors that surprised me less when I learned
more about Mr. J. C. Finklea, the eccentric schoolteacher
who was the census enumerator for Fairhope that year.
Unfortunately, the 1890 census has perished, but the
censuses of 1870 and 1880 told me much more about her
and her family.

These tantalizing fragments only made me hope to
find more. In a public corridor of the county courthouse, carelessly piled in no particular order—un-
tended, their great value unappreciated—I found many
but not all of the county tax records I wanted. There
was some startling information in them. The deed
books, land books, and records of sales of real estate for
nonpayment of taxes were better guarded, and also re-
vealing. Back in the colony archives, I found quitclaims,
references to several different Lewises, all somehow
connected to Nancy, and a reminiscence with a description of the Lewis homestead. As I gathered and put the

information in place a picture began to form. Finally, after I had gone about as far as I could in the public record, I asked a friend if she thought there might be one of Nancy Lewis's descendants to whom I could talk. There was. Rosetta Lewis, the eleventh and youngest child of William Alfred Lewis, Nancy's firstborn, had strong memories of her grandmother as well as of her parents, aunts, uncles, brothers, sisters, and cousins—memories which she generously shared with me. There was also a family Bible in which we could check some of my carefully gathered genealogical data.

Nancy Lewis was born a slave, probably on a farm or plantation, in Lauderdale County, Mississippi, in 1841. Her father had been born in the District of Columbia and her mother in Tennessee. We have no way of knowing when Nancy met her future husband, John. Three years older than she, he was born near Richmond, Virginia, a son of Virginia-born parents. John may have done something to stir his master's wrath—irascible planters sometimes turned their ungrateful slaves over to the slave traders as a means of punishment—or he may have been sold South with his mother as part of his owner's strategy to recover from financial losses, a recourse one Virginia master has described graphically as *his* only means of escaping slavery. In any case, John's experience was hardly unique, for thousands of Virginia slaves were sold to the cotton planters of the lower South in the antebellum years. Somehow John and Nancy met and were married, in whatever ritual sanctioned by their owner, when Nancy was still a teenager and John hardly much more. The family Bible in Rosetta Lewis's living room tells us that their first child, a son named William Alfred, was born in Meridian, Mississippi, on December 18, 1858. The second child, a daughter named Betty—the last Lewis born into slav-

ery—came three years later, after the beginning of the
war that would emancipate her.[16]

As talk of emancipation entered their daily conversa-
tions, Nancy and John Lewis must have thought about
the future with a mixture of elation and apprehension.
Earning a living had to be their first concern. The famous rumor that freedmen were to begin their new
lives with forty acres and a mule, however inaccurately it
foretold federal policy, correctly reflected the unique
importance slaves attached to possession of the land.
For one thing, they had a deep sense that their uncom-
pensated toil had given them a right to the land they
had made productive. In the thousands of pages of
slave testimony that have come down to us, one finds
over and over the moral claim that he who works the
land should reap the benefits of that labor. Slavery had
denied that fundamental principle. Emancipation, if it
were to mean anything, must affirm it. A South Carolina slave put it this way: "The land ought to belong to
the man who . . . *could work it*," not to those who "sit in
the house," profiting from the labor of others.[17] Many
spoke eloquently of the impossibility of freedom without access to the land. To earn a living, rear a family,
gain an education—to live the life of a free man—one
must have land. One of Nancy and John Lewis's fellow
Mississippi slaves put it this way: "Gib us our own land
and we take care ourselves; but widout land, de old
massas can hire us or starve us, as dey please."[18]

A powerful statement of Grandfather's belief that the
"two great questions of chattel slavery and land monopoly . . . are nearer than Siamese twins," these declara-
tions of southern slaves were unvarnished Fairhope philosophy. Henry George asked: "What constitutes the
rightful basis of property?" What was it, he wanted to
know, that justifies one in saying "It is mine!" His

answers echoed the cry of the freedmen: "As a man belongs to himself, so his labor when put in concrete form belongs to him." For this reason, "that which a man makes or produces is his own, as against all the world. . . . No one else can rightfully claim it, and his exclusive right to it involves no wrong to any one else."[19]

A historian of Mississippi tells us that there was a "general belief" among blacks in the autumn of 1865 that "they were to receive land from the government as a Christmas present."[20] If Nancy and John Lewis believed this, they, like other Mississippi freedmen, were soon sorely disappointed. Probably they knew better, for they decided sometime shortly after the end of the war to strike out on their own in fresh territory. Stories reached them of good opportunities in the pine forests of Baldwin County, Alabama, where there had been no plantation tradition. The land was sparsely settled, one might easily find unused acreage for a home and farm site, and the need to extract and distill the sap from the ubiquitous pine trees meant there were good jobs. By the summer of 1870, when the census enumerator came around, John Lewis was employed as a turpentine hand; Nancy was listed as "keeping house" for her husband, their two Mississippi-born children, and the three-month-old baby Mary, their first "freedom child," born on the site that one day would become Fairhope.

"Gib us our own land and we take care ourselves," the Mississippi slave had said. John and Nancy Lewis now set out to prove him right. Precisely how they got their land we shall never know, but a good guess would be that, perhaps on the advice of some of the local blacks they met when they arrived, they simply settled down on land belonging to an absentee owner. The site they chose was part of more than six thousand acres owned by Oscela and Sallie Wilson of Mobile. In 1881 the Wilsons sold these Baldwin County holdings to John Bowen, also of Mobile.[21] Bowen, like the Wilsons, left the land undeveloped. He apparently had no interest in it, except for sport and speculation. One can only surmise that now John Lewis and John Bowen, or Bowen's agent, worked out an agreement—which we may be sure was informal and unwritten—that gave the Lewises use of the land in exchange for payment of the taxes on it. In any case, the incomplete records of tax payments show John—and then Nancy, after John's death in 1891—paying the taxes on eighty acres of land that belonged to John Bowen. For annual levies ranging from $1.35 to $2.33 John and Nancy got their land— eighty acres of it—and set out to look after themselves.[22]

In the Baldwin County wilderness, on the site of the future Fairhope, the young couple had found a good place to start their lives as free people. Eighty acres must have seemed like a dream come true. On fifteen cleared acres they built their home and looked after their animals—a horse, several cows, hogs, and goats (and, no doubt, dogs and cats and chickens, not mentioned in the tax records)—planted vegetables, fruit trees, and vineyards, and reared their family. Three sons—Joseph, John, and James—were born in the seventies. When Betty died in 1883, giving birth to her firstborn, a daughter named Rosa Lee Denton, the granddaughter joined the family, to be reared by Nancy.[23]

There was seldom much extra cash in the household, but work was steady—William Alfred had joined his father as a turpentine hand by 1880—and the farm yielded an abundance of good food. Charles Hall, the tax collector in the 1880s, recalled many years later, when he was a judge and prominent political figure, that riding through Baldwin County was a lonely business. It was a welcome relief to reach the Lewis household. There, day or night, John Lewis would "set me down to the best his farm could yield," which appears to have been both good and memorable.[24] Special family occasions were marked by feasts of freshly roasted hog, according to Rosetta Lewis, who also remembers that her grandmother was a hardworking woman who could plow as well as John Lewis.

In this apparently economically secure world Nancy and John Lewis reared a closely knit and happy family. It is easy to imagine the childhood joys of the Lewis boys and girls. There were deep ravines and endless woods to explore and, less than a mile from home, the sandy beaches and safe waters of Mobile Bay. It was then, as it was to remain for many decades, a children's paradise.

This was the world, too, the single-taxers from the North entered in January of 1895. By that time John Bowen was dead and his heirs were apparently ready to reap the unearned increment from the sale of the Baldwin County lands. The colonists were invited to come to Mobile to talk over terms. No one ever mentioned an agreement with Nancy Lewis, now a widow for the past three years. The estate agent, of course, knew that she had no legal leg to stand on. Nancy, quite understandably, felt differently. Too much of her life was invested in that land to give it up without a protest. She had also just paid the 1894 taxes on the place. It was appraised at $105 and the records show that she owned a horse, ten hogs, five cows, six goats, and personal property valued at $18. William Alfred was married and living nearby; Mary, also married, was living on the place with her husband. Rosa Lee and the boys were still at home. Denying the legal claims of the colonists when they were first shown to her, she soon had no choice but to make plans to start over somewhere else. The law required that she be paid for her improvements—three years of peaceable and undisputed possession of a piece of land were grounds for compensation when dispossession resulted from proof of a better title to the land—and the $100 the colonists paid probably more than met the letter of the law.[25]

➤➤➤✕◄◄◄

What, then, was next for Nancy Lewis? What was to become of her, and her association with my grandfather, as a result of the agreement they both signed in his office?

In June, three months after Nancy had left her old homestead, Grandfather rode his mare Dolly the four miles up to Daphne, the county seat, to attend the annual sale of land for nonpayment of taxes. This was the chance to pick up bargains, and the impecunious colonists needed a lot of these if they were to acquire the land they must have to conduct their demonstration. When he arrived he found that there was one forty-acre parcel, very close to land they already owned, that was on the market. He could foresee the importance this tract would have for the colony and he seemed confident, in his report to the council later, that he could have acquired it. But he decided not to try and he came home empty-handed.

He obviously owed his fellow colonists an explanation. When he arrived at the courthouse, he told them, he met Parker Young, a longtime black resident of the area, and Nancy Lewis. He discovered that the two of them, and their families, were presently living on the very tract now to be sold. They too had ridden up to

Daphne that day—to pay the back taxes so that they might acquire a secure title. Because of what had happened previously between the Fairhope Association and Nancy Lewis, Grandfather told the council, he "did not deem it advisable" to acquire these forty acres. So he stepped aside and came home. And Nancy Lewis became a landowner again, only this time with a legal deed.[26]

Rosetta Lewis, recalling her father's penchant for visiting the courthouse, wondered aloud with me when we talked about this episode if perhaps he had not been there that day. The record of sales of real estate for unpaid taxes proves her right. Those forty acres were sold to him for $4.58. Subsequently, he arranged a transfer of title—properly recorded in the deed book so there could be no displacement this time—assigning twenty acres to his mother and twenty to Parker Young.[27]

Nancy Lewis's new home was less than a mile from her old one. She lived there until she died fifteen years later, at the age of sixty-nine. The value of the land increased steadily. For Nancy Lewis these twenty acres were like a passport to freedom and security, a guarantee that she was fiercely determined to pass on to her children and to Rosa Lee. She subdivided the land—a few old-timers still remember talk of the "Nancy Lewis Subdivision"—and saw to it that her heirs received a legal title to their share. Meanwhile, she supported herself with odd jobs, occasionally as a gardener in Fairhope, continued to eat from her own garden, and accepted the care and support of her children as she grew older. By this time they were managing well on their own, but their mother took pride and satisfaction from knowing that she had given them land that could guarantee their independence in whatever uncertain years might lie ahead.

When she died in July 1910 my grandfather wrote in his newspaper: "Nancy Lewis, one of our old and respected colored citizens, died suddenly Monday morning. At the time Fairhope was founded, she lived in a cabin on what is now the Creswell property but being bought out by the Colony moved a little farther away where she has since lived. She left a large family of children and grandchildren."[28]

TWO

# The Odyssey of Marie Howland

Marie Howland died at The Pines, her Fairhope home, on September 18, 1921, when she was eighty-five years old. For most of her life she was cheerful, effervescent—a happy optimist—but for the previous few years she had been worn down by the struggle against both physical and mental deterioration, "the infirmities of age," my grandfather put it in a long and appreciative obituary he wrote for the *Courier*.[1] She had once jokingly written that her weight problem—her doctor told her she was "too stout by some twenty pounds, or so"—troubled her so that she could "seldom think of death without a sense of mortification that I must give such trouble to my pall bearers!"[2] The many Fairhopers who came to the library for her funeral service, however, would have gladly assumed almost any burden for her, for she was one of their most distinguished comrades and loyal friends. The library, where they gathered to say goodbye to her, was the right place for the service: her extraordinary book collection had formed its nucleus at the beginning and for two decades she had overseen its growth and made it a lively intellectual center for the community of single-taxers, progressive educators, and freethinkers who gathered there.

My grandfather sang at the funeral, as he did on many special occasions in Fairhope. Mrs. Howland had been a good friend almost from the moment she arrived and she had added luster to his newspaper, writing a weekly column of extracts from her letters and serving as associate editor. The colony had no stronger champion than she. For this occasion, Grandfather sang "Only remembered by what we have done," a choice he and Mrs. Howland may have discussed because it was a favorite of reformers and cooperators who believed their lives were important only as they contributed to the struggle for a humane and just social order. "Only the truth that in life we have spoken," one verse went; "only the seed that on earth we have sown; these shall pass onward when we are forgotten, fruits of the harvest and what we have done."

Marie Howland knew her life had been an interesting one and that, even by her own strict standards, there was much for which she should be remembered. "I am quite satisfied to pass off life's stage," she wrote to an old friend some years before her death. It pained her, however, to think of dying without having written an account of her life, and now she did not think that would be possible. "I am not vain nor foolish when I say that it would prove readable to a good class of readers, and give pleasure to the many who have known me," she wrote.[3] It would also have been a major autobiography in the literature of American reform. Grandfather's dignified obituary outlined the theater of her activities—Lowell cotton mills; New York radical and literary salons; an industrial utopia in France; a rural New Jersey command post of reform agitation and happy living; a colony in Mexico devoted to "integral cooperation"; and, finally, the single-tax enclave in Fairhope—

and alerted her future biographer to the many ways in which she had touched great nineteenth-century issues. All the while, as he wrote, she had shown "great force of character," "superior mental ability," and a "remarkable devotion to the cause of humanity."

Six decades after her death Marie Howland is little known outside Fairhope, although signs of interest in her career are popping up here and there. Ray P. Reynolds, one of the first to write about her, has been collecting Howland letters for a long time and he wrote admiringly of her in his book about the cooperative colony in Mexico where she spent five years. Robert S. Fogarty, an authority and frequent commentator on utopian experiments, wrote an introduction to a recently published new edition of her 1874 utopian novel in which he stresses her advocacy of radical reform through cooperative organization. Lynda Morgan, the first scholar to study her Fairhope career and consequently to see her life whole, deftly shows how the various strands of her experience came together in Fairhope so that she felt justified in her life as a "career reformer." Most recently, the imaginative and influential architectural historian Dolores Hayden has featured Howland as one of a significant group of "material feminists" who advocated a "grand domestic revolution." She stands out for her advocacy of cooperative living, kitchenless homes, and scientific child-rearing as means of liberating women from household drudgery and male exploitation.[4]

In Fairhope today few people know much more about her than her name. That has been kept in currency for many years by the Marie Howland Room of the Fairhope Public Library, a center for public meetings and literary activities. When the library was moved to a new building early in 1983, however, no part of it was named after its illustrious pioneer leader. The old-timers who remem-

ber Marie Howland are likely to recall the exotic side of
her character. One octogenarian has a hazy memory of
her as the woman who "led some marches around town
for some radical cause." Another remembers that she
was "kind of odd," but that, "in spite of all her oddness,
she was a brilliant woman." Above all, she was independent: "She just had her own way of doing everything; . . .
she didn't do anything because someone else did it."[5]
The story one hears most frequently—it seems an endur-
ing piece of Howland folklore—is of her scurrying about
town with her coal scuttle, competing with Professor
James Bellangee for cow and horse dung, each of them
devoted to sanitary streets and good gardening.

Though Marie Howland is largely forgotten in Fairhope, her image can still evoke a strong moral point.
Not long ago, for example, a strong-willed and independent female librarian took on the male city fathers in a
contest of wills over her decision to include in the library's holdings a best-selling book on lovemaking techniques. The controversy became interesting enough to
attract a *New Yorker* writer who came down to investigate—and to invoke the memory of Marie Howland to
question the heavy-handed ways of the mayor and
council. After all, he wrote, the Fairhope Public Library
was started by a woman who was "a nineteenth-century
free thinker who had lived for a time in a cooperative
rooming house of a New York free-love advocate, had
written a novel considered too sexually outspoken for
the Boston Public Library, and had begun the Fairhope
collection with books she hauled back from a utopian
community of crédit foncier zealots in Topolobampo,
Mexico." This was not the "sort of library history that
one might expect to find in Opelika or Eufaula," the
writer correctly concluded, pointedly wondering about
the vitality of Fairhope's heritage.[6]

Such was the woman who arrived in Fairhope on March 1, 1899, shortly after the single-tax colony had celebrated its fourth anniversary. There were fewer than a hundred persons living in the community, but Marie sensed immediately a feeling of permanence and vitality. The quality of life was more than she had dared hope for. "You will say this life is idyllic," she wrote to one friend. "I sometimes ask myself if I have not awakened to a better world." She raved about her gardening, where she said her success was "phenomenal," and pronounced Fairhope unique in her experience for its "true freedom" and its "feeling of good fellowship." It was an altogether happy feeling: "I am beginning to love Fairhope," she wrote, "and to feel more at home than I have for many years."[7] These springtime judgments, formed in the first weeks after her arrival, grew stronger as she came to know the community well and to become an important part of it. Her sense of good fortune and well-being perhaps had many sources; one of the main ones was the fact that membership in the Fairhope community turned out to be precisely what she needed to pull together the various strands of her life and to validate her lifelong commitment to communitarian reform.

How had that commitment emerged? What forms had it taken? What were the main themes of Marie Howland's life, the strands she was to weave together in Fairhope? What had her search been about? What did she find?

Hannah Maria Stevens was born on January 23, 1836, in Lebanon, New Hampshire, a farming community of about seventeen hundred people. A bright child from a

poor family, Hannah learned the alphabet from her
older brother when she was two, was taught to form her
letters by her father writing on birch bark with a pin,
and was known by the townspeople as a child hungry
for learning. When she was eight she began selling wild
strawberries in the village, "coveting above all things the
books that were for sale," she later wrote, "and which
my father's poverty placed far beyond my reach." Some
of her memories of those days were happy ones—"the
stolen boat, the sails on the Connecticut River, pine
stumps ablaze and children standing roasting ears of
corn by the fire"—but others were of a childhood she
called "unhappy, neglected." When she was twelve her
father died. By then she had five-year-old twin sisters,
Ada and Melissa, and much of the care of them fell to
her. There would be no more schooling. Unable to cope
with the financial disaster upon them, the family scat-
tered. For a brief period Hannah appears to have been
in Manchester, New Hampshire, living in a boardinghouse along with twenty-seven other girls and young
women. Manchester was a textile center, and Hannah
may well have been working in one of the local mills.
Not yet fifteen, she was making her own way toward
economic independence and having her first experience with a sisterhood of fellow workers in the board-
ing-house of Reuben Page and his wife. Ada and Melissa were separated from her, living with relatives.[8]

From Manchester Hannah went to Lowell, Massachusetts, the textile capital of New England and one of
the wonders of the burgeoning industrial world. For a
generation youngsters like her had been making their
ways to the Lowell dormitories and mills. "From the
farms of Massachusetts, Vermont, New Hampshire,
and Maine came robust young women," one historian
writes, "lured by the highest wages offered to female

employees anywhere in America." The girls and young women became an industrial labor force to be reckoned with as time passed and, much to the surprise of the industrialists who had planned the mill villages, the boardinghouses where they lived became hatcheries of a new consciousness: "the closely knit community of female workers living together created new values, solidarity, and political activism."[9] Hannah did not live in one of the dormitories—she was with her mother and her older brother in Lowell—and female radicalism in the mills had begun to taper off by the time she arrived, in the early 1850s, in part because the owners were changing their earlier preference for Yankee girls to immigrants, especially the Irish, who could be hired for lower wages. From what we know of her later, however, Hannah must have imbibed the radical spirit, with its energizing sense of sisterhood. She certainly took great pride in her work, later telling her husband that she had taken charge of four looms at a time, working as a weaver thirteen hours a day. She also began to write in Lowell—juvenile pieces published in the local papers—and she chose the name Marie as her nom de plume. From that time on, everyone but her grandmother called her Marie.[10]

From Lowell Marie moved on to Boston. One source—not entirely reliable—reports that she was writing for the Boston papers when she was seventeen, which would have been in 1853, while she was "a student in the Phrenological office of Fowlers & Wells at Boston, and managed also to learn the art of Phonography [Pitman shorthand], being able at 18 to report a sermon or speech very thoroughly."[11] By the time she was nineteen she was in New York, on her own, and on the verge of extraordinary experiences.

She must have tried her hand at several jobs in the

first months after her arrival. We know that she spent some time addressing wrappers. Soon, however, she found work in the most dismal part of the city, the infamous Five Points area of the Sixth Ward. Charles Dickens had visited this place a decade earlier and reported that "in respect of filth and wretchedness" it matched the worst slums in London. Visiting one of the "hideous tenements" he found that "from every corner, as you glance about you in these dark retreats, some figure crawls half-awakened, as if the judgment hour were at hand." Described by a modern historian as "the most depraved few acres in North America," the Five Points teemed with bars, dance halls, houses of prostitution— and desperate people. By the early 1850s the Ladies' Home Missionary Society had established a mission there, providing religious instruction, food and shelter, rudimentary job training, and schooling for the young. The ladies of the mission reported in 1854 that they hoped to rescue as many of the children as possible "from the almost certain result of corrupt parental example." Marie Stevens became one of the teachers on whom the ladies of the mission pinned their hopes. "My first experience in teaching in New York was in the Mission School," Marie later wrote. Here she came to learn frightening new lessons about the degradation of poverty and the meaning of hopelessness. Her appointment was as a teacher, but she often found herself helping out in other ways—"ministering to the waifs brought in . . . out of school hours," as she put it.[12]

Perhaps seeking an antidote to the brutal real world of the Five Points slums, Marie was drawn to the fantasy world of the theater. In the fall of 1855, when she was nineteen, she made her debut, as an amateur, on the New York stage. Her talents were modest, and no one encouraged her to develop them.[13] But Marie's theater fling had other important consequences for her education. Most important of all, she met and became an intimate friend of a fellow nineteen-year-old, a rare beauty from Charleston who burst upon the New York stage and scene in 1855. Giving herself the name "Ada Clare," Jane McElhenney had come up from South Carolina to make her way as an actress, a writer, and—as it turned out—the "Queen of Bohemia." A dazzling woman who graced the society of young journalists, writers, artists, actors, and radicals—the avant-garde of New York social and intellectual life—the vivacious and unconventional Ada must have given Marie a measure of confidence as she opened her eyes to new ways of living. Ada's other special friend in the autumn of 1855 was the Louisiana composer and pianist Louis Moreau Gottschalk, with whom she had a notorious affair. She wrote about her love in the *New York Atlas* and then sailed for Paris early in 1857 to bear their son when Gottschalk ruled out marriage.[14] Marie doubtless gave support to Ada during her turmoil, just as she would provide a sanctuary for her and her son Aubrey in later years. "My beautiful Ada Clare," she wrote of her friend, "whose strange heart-history will never be written, perhaps, was a brilliant, lovable woman, rather imperious, as great beauties are apt to be, but noble, affectionate, tender, and very honorable and exact in all her dealings."[15]

Marie's education and range of stimulating acquaintances were expanded by her visits in 1855 to a place called The Club. "I was several times at the Club 555 Broadway," she later recalled in a confidential letter to an old friend from those days.[16] The Club was the brainchild of Stephen Pearl Andrews, one of the most interesting of the iconoclastic spirits and magnetic personalities who contributed to Marie's education. An anarchist whose slogan "Individual Sovereignty" bespoke a quest for personal liberation, Andrews began The Club in a small hall on Bond Street. Its popularity forced a move to more commodious quarters over Taylor's Saloon at 555 Broadway.[17] At twice-weekly meetings the rooms would be filled with a fascinating variety of humanity—come to dance, play parlor games, receive instruction in French, make the acquaintance of other partisans of "Individual Sovereignty," and talk about the new social order. Albert Brisbane, the chief American popularizer of Charles Fourier, was a friend of Andrews and a frequent visitor. The aim of The Club, Brisbane explained to New Yorkers, was to establish the "right of every individual to be the sole judge of his or her own actions, and to follow the dictates of his or her own attractions, provided it did not infringe upon the rights of others." Man's right to *think* for himself had long been established and was everywhere accepted, he declared. What now must be accepted—what The Club existed to forward—was the "right of the individual to feel for himself, to follow his attractions." That right was "condemned by the moralists as immoral and vicious," Brisbane wrote, but those so-called moralists were mistaken.[18]

Mistaken or not, they had a great deal to say about The Club in the fall of 1855. Both the *Times* and the *Tribune* ran long stories purporting to describe what went on above Taylor's Saloon. The *Tribune* reported that "so rapid has been its growth that the name 'Free-Love' is now on the lips of every body."[19] The *Tribune* reporter no doubt exaggerated, but it is true that Marie arrived in New York just as the free-love movement was beginning to flourish and that at The Club she heard it debated, defended, and explained. She met some persons who were later to be called "varietists," holding that "love, like lust, was general rather than specific in its objects, and therefore it naturally sought plurality and variety in its arrangements."[20] Marie was drawn to the side of those who would be called the exclusivists, maintaining that love, which should be the only basis for marriage, was incompatible with "plurality and variety." For most of her idealistic new friends, free love stood as the antithesis of slave love; it meant that women should be liberated from male domination, free to form marriage on the basis of love, dissolve it in the absence of love, and offer or withhold their bodies on their own terms. This kind of free-love doctrine naturally merged with the feminism that inspired her acquaintances and was to become central to her own life as a communitarian reformer.

One of the young idealists Marie met at The Club was destined to have a special role in her education. He was Lyman W. Case, a Harvard graduate from Winsted, Connecticut. They were married when Marie was twenty-one and Lyman not much older. As Dolores Hayden aptly puts it, Case "played Henry Higgins to her Eliza Doolittle."[21] Years later she wrote to their mutual friend Edmund Clarence Stedman recalling how "Mr. Case was always coaching me in speech, manners, movements . . . & I was very grateful for the pains he took." Like Eliza Doolittle, however, Marie had her trying moments. She recalled the time she cried out in despair, "I do not know how to please you. . . . I do not seem to know how to do anything properly."[22] On the whole, though, she was pleased. "I owe much to the training of Mr. Case," she wrote Stedman on another occasion, specifying in particular the way he put her "through the course of logic of the Fordham school for

priests, using a Latin text book when I did not know a
hundred words in Latin." Case must have been a good
teacher because Marie was "astonished to find it absolutely easy after the first obstacles were passed."[23]

Perhaps most important of all, Case helped his young
wife to work her way to a comprehensive world view, a
system of thought into which she could fit her remarkable experiences, her increasingly penetrating insights,
and her emerging reformist sensibilities. Like most intellectuals at The Club, Case was a disciple of Fourier,
the Frenchman who had identified the great crisis of his
age as the failure of men to find satisfaction in their
work and in their emotional relationships. His complex
and often baffling writings pointed the way to a resolu-
tion of the crisis and opened up for his followers a world
of breathtaking possibilities. Many rejected Fourier—or
simply dismissed him—because of his turgid prose, his
crammed stable of new words and phrases, and such
bizarre notions as the purification of the seas and the
copulation of the planets. More picked up on and dis-
torted a few of his phrases—"passional attraction," for
example—and labeled him the worst of free-lovers,
bent on subverting Western civilization. They were
partly right in this, for Fourier believed that civilization
was corrupt, could not be saved by reform, but must be
replaced by new values, relationships, modes of work,
recreation, and education that could only be nurtured
in a new social unit to which he gave the name "phalanx." A phalanx was a precisely designated small community of a specified number of people who would live
in new architectural creations called "phalansteries."
Change would come about not through violence and
revolution, but as a consequence of a successful series of
exemplary phalanxes. Thus, even within the repressive
order of, say, New York in the 1850s, Fourier's disciples

could find constructive things to do: they could study and propagate his ideas, and they could search for their own ways of translating those ideas into communitarian experiments, a move that had several precedents already.[24]

Fourier's thought radiated from a faith that it was possible to create an environment in which disparate and antagonistic elements could be united, brought into harmony. All one needed to do was understand instinctive human drives—the givens of human nature that he called "passional attractions." Fourier discovered twelve of these, and he claimed that the system he built on them—his world of phalanxes and phalansteries—required no alterations of human nature. As one scholar puts it, "Fourier's discovery of the divine formula for the correct arrangement of human passions permitted all to follow exactly and entirely the inclinations of their natures and yet in the process add their share to perfect social harmony."[25] Fourier must have been especially appealing to a cheerful reformer like Marie who shied away from violence and deplored revolution. The appeal lay in his plan to unite rather than divide capitalists and laborers and in his vision of a world in which hierarchy would continue to exist, but on a foundation of recognized merit, not deplored exploitation. Capitalists, for example, would learn that profit sharing was in their interest materially as well as morally and laborers, blossoming in the ingenious schemes for variety at the work place, would come to enjoy their labors. Sharing profits, taking pride in the work that was done, and participating in the great panoply of cultural, intellectual, and social benefits of the phalanstery, everyone would have a stake in the society and wish to maintain and replicate it.

Soon after they were married, Lyman and Marie Case

moved into a household that was conceived as a practical application of Fourier's teachings. Case and Andrews and a few others founded what they called, in good Fourierist language, the "Unitary Household," a cooperative boardinghouse on Stuyvesant Street that they hoped would be the rough equivalent of a phalanstery. Twenty persons moved into the large four-story brick structure in May 1858. Each family had a private suite, but all the residents came together in the public parlors to take meals, hold discussions, and enjoy Saturday-night dancing. Stedman, who moved in that fall with his wife and child, later wrote that the "Unitary scheme" called for no profit on rent, food, or service— which made it a great bargain—and that it attracted more than its share of interesting people, both as residents and as visitors. It was a time, Stedman recalled, when "visions were beheld, and the questioning spirit was abroad."[26] A sympathetic *New York Times* reporter believed these "Free-Lovers" had cut living costs by a third as they began to do "what Mr. Charles Fourier . . . vainly attempted to accomplish—unite different families, under a single system of regulations," and "live cheaply" as well. The result, he concluded, was that these former denizens of The Club had introduced into the "heart of New York, without noise or bluster, a successful enterprise based on Practical Socialism."[27]

A later *New York Times* account was less sympathetic. A journalist seized by hysteria claimed that the Stuyvesant Street Unitary Household "was founded as a theater for the exercise of the pernicious and lustful passions which the doctrine of 'Free Love' engenders." As a "practical application of the Free-Love doctrine," he announced, "it was more than successful; it was a positive triumph of Lust."[28] Stedman's memory ran less to the dramatic. "There were as many romances, and jealousies, as elsewhere," he recalled.[29] Marie Stevens Case was a principal figure in one of the "practical applicatio⌐ ɔ" of the "free-love doctrine" at the Unitary Household, and she later wrote about it candidly.

One evening, Marie explained, Henry Clapp, Jr., the brilliant editor of a new literary publication in town, came calling at the household with a friend. Both of them were ardent Fourier men. There was piano music, Marie recalled, and everyone began dancing, marching around the "big old double parlors." Her partner was the guest brought by Henry Clapp. They kept dancing. "At length someone pulled my skirt to remind me that the march had ceased and all were seated—all but Edward Howland and myself who were quite lost to all the environment." After the guests had left, Marie and her husband retired to their room. Case said to her: "Marie, you have met your destiny." She protested that in Case she surely had already met her destiny. He interrupted her: "No lying, Marie. You have met the man of all men whom you need."[30]

Fourier taught that "the attractions are proportionate to the destinies."[31] Marie and Edward Howland had displayed an unmistakable spiritual affinity that evening, a passional attraction that Case said he recognized as the destiny for each of them. He was not mistaken. Edward and Marie fell deeply in love, and Case withdrew to remain a lifelong friend of both.[32]

The charming Edward Howland, like Marie's friend Ada Clare, was born in Charleston, where his Mayflower-descendant father was a cotton merchant. As a teenager he moved north for schooling, in New York and Boston. He studied at Harvard College, graduating

in 1853. Lyman Case was his classmate. When he met
Marie he was twenty-six and she just twenty-three. Since
his graduation he had worked for his father's cotton
brokerage firm, representing it on Wall Street or looking after business for brief periods in Boston, Memphis,
and New Orleans. He had also begun to collect books
and apparently assembled a valuable collection which he
sold in order to finance a new literary venture, the *New
York Saturday Press,* which began publication in October
1858 under the editorship of Henry Clapp, Jr., the
friend who had brought him to the Unitary Household
to meet his "destiny." According to one source, Clapp
converted Edward to Fourier.[33] He was certainly a zealous disciple when Marie met him, and his enthusiasm
fortified Marie's own commitment. "No person who was
mentally capable of stating the doctrine of Fourier ever
doubted any of its great fundamental truths," Edward
assured her. Edward also believed that, "among all the
friends of women, none was so great as Fourier, for no
others believed in her absolute freedom." As a burgeoning feminist, Marie applauded such a view, just as she
did Edward's conviction, which he said was derived
from Fourier, that "as long as man has power to hold
woman by any tie but that of the love he inspires, he will
not know the depth, the tenderness nor the upholding
power of her affection for him as a man." Free to love—
to let love form the basis of marriage—Marie left her
first husband with his approval and with the self-confidence inspired by the prophet Fourier in whom all
three of them believed. And she was fortunate in her
love. "No man," she would later write of Edward, "could
be more delicately respectful of woman's nature, her
rights, and even her whims and wishes."[34]

   Not long after her first march about the big old
double parlors of the Unitary Household, Marie moved

out. The household itself had been a great success—so much so that much larger quarters were secured elsewhere to accommodate more boarders. Marie, however, set up on her own. She brought to New York her teenage sister Ada, who had recently divorced the father of her newborn child. Ada looked after Marie's small house while Marie pursued her career as an educator.[35] She had left the Mission House school for the public school system and for over two years she had been studying on Saturday mornings at the Normal School. She found her studies "the happiest part of my life up to that time," she later wrote.[36] In July of 1859 she received her certificate, graduating with "highest records."[37] After a brief period as assistant principal in an elementary school she took over for several years as principal of Public School No. 11, located in what Edward called a "rough quarter" of the city. She was a sympathetic and imaginative teacher and, at least according to Edward, she knew the names of every one of her five hundred pupils.[38] In addition to her professional competence as a teacher, Marie had also learned Pitman's shorthand so that by the time she and Edward began seeing each other she had acquired the basis for that economic independence she believed women must have to be truly free. As Lynda Morgan writes, her accomplishments were "remarkable for a lower class girl of the mid-nineteenth century."[39]

Meanwhile, she continued to broaden her horizons in New York social and intellectual circles. The new publication sponsored by Edward and edited by Clapp lasted only two years, but it sparkled for that time and attracted to it some of the best young writers of the day. They were dubbed Bohemians both for their unconventional ways of living and for their iconoclastic writings. William Winter, who lived with Edward on Bleecker

Street for a while and was Clapp's assistant editor, wrote that "the purpose of 'The Saturday Press' was to speak the truth, and . . . cast ridicule upon as many as possible of the humbugs then extant and prosperous in literature and art."[40] Stedman judged the paper to be "irregularly clever," while Marie pronounced it "rather brilliant and very sententious."[41] At a time when the nation was on the verge of civil war, Clapp showed only disdain for politics and never mentioned the slavery controversy. "The Saturday Press has no politics," he boasted. "It looks upon politicians, of whatever breed or half-breed, shell or half-shell, as an uninteresting species of maniac."[42] Among the many bright contributors to this lively new voice in the city were George Arnold, Edward G. B. Wilkins, Ada Clare, Fitz-James O'Brien, Thomas B. Aldrich, and Walt Whitman. In the evenings they gathered for drink and conversation at Pfaff's Cellar, the favored haunt of the writers, actors, playwrights, artists, and critics of New York Bohemia. Ada Clare, back some time from Paris with her son Aubrey, presided here.[43]

In her old age Marie could recall only one visit to Pfaff's, an occasion when she asked Edward to take her. She claimed that she was really not one of the coterie of Bohemians, but she knew them all, sharpened her wits in conversation with them, and saw most of them frequently at the Sunday evening "informal, unconventional literary receptions" at Ada Clare's home on Forty-second Street. They were "a very choice circle of friends," she recalled. Ada Clare was especially important to her. "I always went on Sat. night," before the Sunday parties, she wrote, "and shared her room & bed."[44]

By the time the Civil War broke out, Marie had completed a major phase of her education. Rich in experiences, intimately acquainted with the wretched and the deprived as well as the glittering and the privileged, professionally trained as a teacher and a stenographer, polished as a conversationalist, she had worked out a critique of civilization and grasped a vision of a better world. She had also found the man she loved. Now she and Edward had to consider their future together.

Neither of them was seriously touched by the controversy over slavery or the war that resulted from it. Although he was reared in South Carolina, Edward felt no loyalty to the South, and Marie, spiritually allied to the abolitionists, sensed no urgency to bolster the Union cause. Marching to a different drummer, they set off for Europe. Edward was by this time a well-known bibliophile and he traveled for the New York firm of Philes & Company (as the "& Co.," Marie later wrote) scouting for old books. Marie resigned her principalship at Public School No. 11 and in February 1863 set sail for England on the steamer *Teutonia*. She was back in the States in 1864, summering on Long Island with Ada Clare, while Edward came out for weekends. She returned to Britain in the summer of 1865. By this time the divorce had come through. She and Edward were married in Sterling, Scotland, on August 12, 1865. He was almost thirty-three; she, twenty-nine. After the wedding they enjoyed a "romantic journey accomplished on the top of an omnibus," during which Edward read Scott's poetry "as we passed places immortalized by that poet of youth and romance," as Marie described their honeymoon.[45]

The Howlands came home from their European travels in 1866 with a treasury of good memories. They had settled down for brief periods in London and Amsterdam, and they had toured England, Scotland, and the Continent. Edward added notably to his personal collec-

tion of valuable books and Marie, now determined to be
an author, gathered information and impressions for
articles she would write. By far their most important
experience was the discovery of a working example of
Fourier's phalanstery—an example that was to be a lifelong inspiration for both of them.[46]

At Guise, France, a successful iron industrialist who
designed and manufactured stoves had created a "social
palace" for his large work force. His name was Jean-
Baptiste André Godin and he welcomed Edward and
Marie to his Familistère. The Familistère was the unique
home of the men, women, and children who were associated with Godin's factory. Marie and Edward were understandably dazzled by it. Godin explained how, in the
first half of the century, "capital and labor created the
great industries and revolutionized our methods of
transportation." For the next half century, he believed,
"the work to be done . . . is to effect a grand reform in the
architecture of the home." He rejected the idea that the
crisis in relations between labor and capital and the mis-
erable standards of living for most working people could
be ameliorated by strategies based on antagonism radiat-
ing from families living in "isolated homes." Poverty and
hopelessness were the "essential accompaniment" of the
laborer's environment, Godin believed. His aim—and
the challenge of the future—was "to change the environment." The Familistère was founded to do just that: "Not
being able to make a château of the tenement . . . we have
sought to unite the homes of many workmen in one *palace*. The Familistère is the palace home of Labor—the
SOCIAL PALACE of the future."[47]

Still in the process of construction when they discovered it, the Familistère must nonetheless have seemed to
Edward and Marie the perfect proof of Fourier's doctrine that life and work could be so integrated as to make

possible a harmonious social order in which men and women found satisfaction in both their labor and their emotional relationships. In the factory, located on the east bank of the Oise River, the workers seemed enthusiastic about what they were doing, and the Howlands believed this was a natural consequence of profit sharing, communal decisions about working hours and conditions, and the inspired leadership of Godin. Across the river was the Familistère. Surviving pictures and architectural drawings suggest Godin did not exaggerate when he called it a social palace. More than anything else it might remind the modern American of a combination condominium, elegant shopping mall, neighborhood garden, and futuristic school building—all run cooperatively and for the benefit of everyone. Much of the daily domestic routine—cooking, laundry, child care—was socialized, carried on cooperatively, a feature of the Familistère that especially impressed Marie. The education of the children, as Edward put it, "commences from the cradle." Infants could be kept in their private apartments, but he observed that most mothers sent their very young children to the nursery and that from then on their education and the organization of the right conditions for their growth were major responsibilities of the Familistère. Based on the educational theories of Fourier and Froebel—Edward called it "integral education"—the schools of the Familistère had much in common with what Marie was to discover later in Fairhope's "organic" school.[48]

Back in New York, Edward and Marie found a pleasant home at the corner of Ninth Avenue and Twenty-second Street. Edward worked for *Leslie's Illustrated Weekly Magazine* for a short while and also wrote a campaign biography of General Grant. Marie worked during the winter of 1867–68 with the stenographic corps

of the New York state constitutional convention. Both
of them churned out magazine articles but, as Marie put
it, "not enough were accepted to keep us." A "season of
much anxiety" set in and they made the decision to
move to the country. It was among the happiest decisions they ever made.[49]

➜➤➤❮❮❮

For the next two decades, Marie and Edward lived in
Hammonton, New Jersey. Not long after they arrived
they acquired a home on twenty-two acres. They called
it Casa Tonti and it became their Shangri-la. They
cleared the land, planted fruits, vegetables, and flowers,
and took enormous pride in their self-sufficiency. In a
story based on their Casa Tonti life Marie wrote of their
"folly in living so long cooped up in the city," and of
their joy in preparing dinners with ingredients "all from
our own place, and with the work of our own hands."[50]
She never ceased to write about the joy she took in gardening, taking special pleasure in her roses, of which
she boasted fifty varieties. To finance their Casa Tonti
existence, Marie and Edward took charge of the local
high school for a while, Marie gave lessons in music and
in French, they kept their expenses down by raising
much of what they needed, and they had a small income
from their writing.

Marie was an ebullient woman with an almost unlim-
ited range of interests. She could write with equal fervor
about flowers and feminism, and the enthusiasm she
had for the study of child-rearing spilled over into essays and stories on bee culture, climate control, nutrition, scientific music notation, Japanese education,
peace, violence, and war. In articles on politics, such as
her discussion of the Grange movement which she and

Edward joined, she lauded the fact that "men and women are received on terms of absolute equality." She could turn a detailed discussion of the latest methods of chicken raising into a feminist argument, pointing out that the successful career of one woman with an advanced hatchery "was another instance in proof of the fact that the business qualities of women were rapidly asserting themselves." And she drew a pointed moral: "Say what we may of the beauty of dependence in women, dependence is not charming except in weak and inferior creatures." Women had "tasted the forbidden fruit of pecuniary independence in many fields," she warned, and they were not to be turned back.[51]

Her major achievement as a writer was her novel *Papa's Own Girl,* written at Casa Tonti and published in 1874. The *Harper's* reviewer greeted it enthusiastically, praising its "utmost delicacy of treatment" and its "frequent touches of humor." More important, he believed that "no novel has yet appeared so comprehensive in its range, bearing upon the great social questions of the day, the position of woman and the conditions of labor."[52] The reviewer was right about these being Marie's major concerns and her romantic utopian novel became the vehicle for an elaborate statement of them. Drawing on her experience at Guise, she resolved the labor problem of the novel by bringing to the New England town in which it was set (a village modeled on Lebanon) a Count von Fraunstein (which means "ladies' rock") to establish a Familistère like Godin's. The count brings with him not only his cooperative social schemes but his feminist convictions as well. "I am always on the side of women as against men," he declares, adding that women can never be happy "until they are pecuniarily independent." There will be jobs for them at the Familistère, just as there are at Guise.[53]

By the standards of the time *Papa's Own Girl* was a forthright and heretical book and consequently it ran into difficulties. At the Philadelphia Mechanic's Library a clerk confided that "its doctrines are corrupting." It was banned altogether from the Boston Public Library, for its "coarseness": Dr. Forest, the hero of the novel, declares that "the first condition for the development of broad sympathies for humanity in a woman's heart is the loss of respectability as defined by hypocrites and prudes." Equally offensive was Dr. Forest's advice to a "fallen woman" that she should "cultivate the thought that it is not you, but conventional society that makes it wrong to have a child by one you love, and right by one you loathe, if you happen to be married to him." Marie could understand that opposition to the work came from these feminist, free-love quotations, but she wrote that fear was also aroused by the novel's cooperationist doctrine and the moral she had learned from Godin that "wealth owes a duty to the disinherited of the earth which cannot be discharged by merely paying wages or by giving alms." More bluntly, she explained the public's fears to E. H. Cheney, the editor of her old hometown newspaper in Lebanon, who had discovered her and made her into something of a local celebrity:

It is too radical; there is the trouble; for it tends, not only to show that there can be no wise and successful government without equality of civil and political rights for all citizens, but to show that industry is wronged and robbed when the industrious poor are compelled to live in mean houses without baths or any of the conditions of high culture; when the producers of the wealth and luxury of the world are unable, even after a life of unremitting drudgery, to afford their children an efficient education; unable to secure leisure for study and recreation; unable in fact to raise themselves by honest labor alone, above the life of the drudge, or to make it certain that they can escape dependence upon the charity of their relations or the horrors of the poorhouse when misfortune arises, or when disabled by old age.[54]

By the mid-seventies Marie was established as a prominent feminist novelist and an articulate propagandist for a cooperative society. She had met stimulating intellectuals and reformers in Europe and America, she was unusually well read in many fields, and she and Edward had helped each other to refine and perfect their thoughts as only a communicative and supportive couple can. They were also leading an idyllic life. Many of their old radical friends from New York visited them so that there was a constant flow of interesting people and good conversation. Ada Clare spent most of her summers there, until her tragic death in 1874.[55] Among new friends was Victoria Woodhull, the free-love advocate, celebrity, and 1872 presidential candidate. Perhaps most important of all was the lush setting of fruits and flowers, a constant source of pleasure, and the fact that Edward and Marie were deeply in love with each other. Edward, Marie said of him later, was a "*real* husband—friend, comrade, mentor, brother, lover, all in one."[56] The problem was that their good life seemed increasingly unrelated to the injustices of the world they had come to understand so well, and their writings pathetically weak instruments of social change. What they needed was a theater for action, a cause, a program in which they could somehow make a practical demonstration of their theories. When Albert Kimsey Owen entered their lives, that opportunity came.

Owen came to Casa Tonti in 1875 to talk to Marie. He had read *Papa's Own Girl* and he saw in its author an ally for a grandiose scheme hatching in his fertile brain. A railroad engineer with plans for constructing lines to the Pacific, Owen was a dreamer, a socialist, and something of a swashbuckler. Edward and Marie were charmed by him and soon they were helping him to refine his plans and recruit members and raise funds for the great "Pacific City" he hoped to build at Topolobampo in the sunny Mexican province of Sinaloa. Marie immediately saw the chance to make a reality of the imaginary Familistère she had created in her novel, to transplant to the new world the creation of her hero, Godin. "Why not . . . try for the Social Palace?" she wrote to Owen in 1875. Over the next several years they explored the possibilities and apparently sparred over how far to go in socializing domestic services. Marie made her points forcibly; it was "supremely important," she told him, that women be free "from the household treadmill." On another occasion she chided him: "Now Albert, depend upon it, we must allow people who wish to do so to form groups and dine together. Let the cook prepare and all who wish, let them eat at the general table."[57] With the help of a Philadelphia architect they drew up magnificent plans for the new city and it was apparent that Marie had carried most of her points. There were to be commodious residential hotels as well as row houses and separate kitchenless cottages—a melange of living arrangements—all adjoining or close to cooperative housekeeping facilities. As in Guise, the nursery was to occupy a central role—the child-care center which would make possible women's economic independence as well as the educational center that would insure what Owen and Marie (who became director of education) called "integral growth," a term they used to signify growth of the whole person. The plan was completed with a support battery of recreational, cultural, and intellectual facilities. Such was to be the environment of the colony whose motto was Collective Ownership and Management for Public Utilities and Conveniences—The Community Responsible for the Health, Usefulness, Individuality and Security of Each.[58]

In 1885 Owen published a book called *Integral Co-Operation* in which the plans for the colony were laid out.[59] Marie had a major hand in writing it. In that same year she and Edward began the publication of the colony newspaper which they distributed widely to drum up interest in the venture. They also began to make plans to move to Mexico themselves. Edward's health was declining steadily and mysteriously and the burdens on Marie were becoming too great. She saw through to publication in 1886 her translation of Godin's *Solutions Sociales,* of all her works the one of which she was most proud.[60] That finished, she could think about the move to Mexico, hoping the sun would help Edward and the company of fellow cooperators would relieve some of the burden on her. "I rejoice that we are going to Mexico," she wrote to her friend Stedman, explaining that "this life is destroying me. I feel my physical strength, even, giving way." They left Casa Tonti in the spring of 1888. Shortly after their arrival in August, Marie wrote a cheerful letter about the prospects in Mexico. Edward, however, was no better. Less than a year later she wrote: "Edward will not get well I fear. All the doctors give up on him. . . . He walks with much help, totteringly, and is often lost, mentally."[61] He died on Christmas Day, 1890. "I thought I was prepared," she wrote, but she stood there "with feelings no tongue could utter, beside my beloved dead."[62]

Owen described Marie as the "soul" of his colony, but she was never fully accepted by the other colonists. Her natural optimism and her faith in the cause resulted in positive articles on colony life, but from the beginning there were obvious signs of discord. Part of the problem was that the colony never had the funds or the talent

even to begin to build the Familistère. The buildings
and paths that they did construct bore no resemblance
at all to their blueprints. Life was rudimentary and
offered no cushion for the quarrels over company management and the clashes over Marie's unconventional
views and behavior. For her part, Marie privately confessed her disappointment that "there are not here
nearly so many as I had hoped of broad-thinking, lib-
eral people."[63]

Topolobampo was no free-love colony and Marie's
"advanced" ways along with her rumored scarlet past
got her into deep trouble. Totally without guile and
deeply committed to her beliefs, she was an easy target.
She swam nude, took Edward along with her for his
health, and proclaimed what they were doing was enjoy-
able and beneficial. She lashed out at the custom that
made women ride sidesaddle ("we must protect any lady
in her right to use any kind of saddle she chooses"), she
advocated sensible dress, and she insisted that dancing
was essential to wholesome, happy, "integral" development.[64] Her enemies saw all of these things as as-
saults on the moral welfare of the community. One of
the wives got so worked up over the outlandish Marie
that she appealed to her sister colonists to consider
whether they were "willing to have this corrupting influence among us spoiling our girls and boys and even our
married women."[65]

One of the men, once a staunch feminist but now
reduced to what the record makes sound like voyeur-
ism, entered a formal complaint against Marie. He reported that he had seen her

go into the sea from the beach, naked, without any clothing on her
so that I and others saw her entire form, and she swam in company
with men also naked. . . . I saw this many times, sometimes by the full
moon light, sometimes by the waning light of day. . . . She also more

than once walked up to my tent to hang clothes on the ropes to dry, but she had nothing on except her chemise or night dress split part way down in front so that I could see that part of her person that in a decent woman is kept covered from the gaze of men; and she said to my wife, "I guess I won't scare your husband."[66]

Deeply disappointed in her comrades, Marie struck back. As director of education she insisted that dancing, which her opponents had condemned as sexually pro-vocative, was in fact healthy and should be part of the school curriculum. Who could imagine a Familistère without children and adults dancing! When Owen failed to back her in the controversy over women riding astride instead of sidesaddle, Marie poured out her anger at the growing intolerance:

Could you not trust me to not lead our girls into anything unbecom-ing? . . . No, alas! Because . . . in the night, I went into the sea un-dressed! That a woman would dare to bathe her ugly self undressed! My God! When I think that there is no place on earth where our poor sex has any rights that men are bound to respect, I feel that I have toiled and struggled in vain to make the world better for my single effort.[67]

With Edward gone and no hope of making a success out of her commitment to Topolobampo, Marie finally pulled out, leaving in the summer of 1893. She started a period of wandering, visiting old friends and relatives. She began writing fiction again and she gave interviews on her Topolobampo experience, generally putting a gloss on the terrible disappointments she had experi-enced so that she stressed the hopeful features of the colony's history and recalled her numerous interesting experiences and good friends. One of the best of those friends was Christian B. Hoffman, a wealthy Swiss-born Kansan and a principal supporter of the Mexican ven-ture. During his visits to Topolobampo he and Marie had become devoted to each other and now she turned to him for guidance.[68] For some time Hoffman had been subscribing to the *Fairhope Courier* and exchanging letters with my grandfather. He was too firmly rooted in Kansas—with a wife and children and a thriving business—to consider Fairhope as a home for himself, but he suggested that Marie investigate it. It might be just the place for her to nurture her battered convictions and pass the declining years of her life.

Grandfather informed the Fairhopers on July 1, 1898, that an inquiry had come from the well-known Marie Howland, "a very talented woman and an ardent reformer." Through the columns of the *Courier* he let her know she would be "a welcome addition to our community" should she decide to come. Marie replied, full of enthusiasm for the Henry George cause. She wrote that no misfortune to the colony, "except the abandonment of the single tax experiment," would cause her to leave it. She was determined to come.[69]

The Fairhope colonists responded to the news of her decision with enthusiasm and made characteristic preparations for her arrival. In February 1899 the *Courier* announced that the regular Sunday afternoon discussion meetings were now resuming after a lapse during the holidays. In the fall those meetings had ranged over many subjects: natural rights; cooperative colonies; religion and the single tax; and the proposed revision of the Alabama constitution, among others. The next meeting would be conducted by Mrs. Josephine Woods, who planned to read selections from *Papa's Own Girl* so that the colonists might better understand the thinking of their newest prospective member.[70]

Josephine Woods was the vice-president of the asso-

ciation when Marie arrived. She had come to Fairhope
in 1897 to take over the colony school. James Bellangee,
one of the staunchest Fairhopers, recommended her to
Grandfather as "a very pleasant woman and thoroughly
in sympathy with reform ideas," a woman who was "a
suffragist, a populist and a S[ingle] T[axer]." Once on
the grounds she taught the school, joined the county
and local woman's suffrage clubs, was a lively presence
at cultural and social affairs, and, as vice-president, took
her share of responsibility for governing the colony. At
the anniversary celebration in January she spoke on
"The Women of Fairhope." Marie would have liked
what she said. "Owing largely to its women," Mrs.
Woods declared, "Fairhope has begun well, its future is
promising." So long as women continued to "join
hands" in support of its principles, she promised, Fairhope could be certain of becoming the "model community" its founders envisioned.[71]

Mrs. Woods was one of many strong Fairhope women
who made up a sisterhood unlike any Marie had known
before. Married, single, and widowed, they had come
from many parts of the country, bringing with them a
rich background of reform experiences. One was a dynamic WCTU lecturer, two were physicians, several
were teachers, and a few were editors and writers.
There were artists, musicians, theosophists, nutrition-
ists, and physical culturalists among them. Nearly all
had campaigned for their right to vote—a right they
had and took very seriously in Fairhope. All were
steeped in the philosophy of Henry George. The cor-
nerstone of that philosophy was what they called "the
law of equal freedom," a law that meant, among other
things, equal rights for women.[72]

Strongly committed to political equality, Fairhope
women played a major role in shaping the character of

the community. For one thing they were integrated into the decision-making process of the association almost from the beginning. There were no women among the original officers chosen in Iowa, but all that changed the moment the colonists arrived in Alabama. Three women were elected to office then and two months later Amelia Lamon was chosen vice-president. Women were never a majority on the council but the association was never without women officers. Equally important, the women reminded their male comrades that there would be no backsliding and sometimes they gave lessons in what we would today call consciousness raising. The constitution provided that the spouse of a member could vote without paying the membership fee. Carrie Sykes, a widow, objected because she believed this subordinated wives to husbands. "Are there women in this association who would give up their own identity and individuality?" she thundered. Better that the fee should be lowered and every person pay it. "I say, let us have perfect equality to men and women in the every day working principles and practice, as well as in theory."[73] Such outspoken and firm leadership set a community pattern that was not broken for many decades. Women sat on the Colony Council and those who did not felt no hesitation in dropping in on the council's weekly public meetings where they expected to be taken as seriously as the men.

Formal council meetings were not the only place where influence was exerted and policy made. Almost from the beginning the settlers began the custom of coming together on Sunday afternoons to discuss social, economic, political, and philosophical questions. In time they called these meetings their "Progressive League," which Marie said was the church of the Fairhope colony. Here, in meetings in their hall or on the bluff overlooking the bay, what was said often crystallized community sentiment and helped to shape the way policy matters would be brought before the council. Women not only attended league meetings regularly but they spoke up and were themselves often the speakers. Their topics ranged from Alice Herring's discussion of Buddhism and Socialism to Altona Chapman's explication of techniques for calculating economic rent.[74] The *Courier* reports of these and other meetings, along with colony correspondence and the reminiscences of the early settlers, suggest that personality and force of argument, rather than gender, determined who made public policy in Fairhope.

This was, of course, a happy discovery for Marie and she both strengthened and celebrated the role of women in Fairhope politics and public life. Marie also found that her Fairhope sisters were unusually active club women. The Progressive League and the Library Review Club (which she started) were for all members of the community, but the women organized for themselves the Ladies' Henry George Club, the Women's Single Tax Club, the Woman's Suffrage Society; the Women's Social Science Club, the Village Improvement Club, the Women's Christian Temperance Union, and the Fifth Thursday Club, a confederacy of all women's club members. "We are becoming a club town," Marie wrote, "women's clubs especially."[75] These Fairhope club women sewed, drank tea, and exchanged recipes at their gatherings, but the brain power and moral energy they expended were on genderless questions of social, economic, and political reform as well as on the special role women ought to play in reforming the larger social order. Before she came to Fairhope, Marie had written that women were so "wronged and robbed by law and by custom" and so "handicapped in the struggle of life" that they turned to women's clubs "just as the down-trodden wage workers"

turned to unions.[76] Now, in Fairhope, she could see some
of the fruit of that action. Here in the Fairhope clubs
women found strength and personal satisfaction. They
also used the clubs as forums for the discussion and perfection of ideas that might later be presented to the council for action. In many ways, as Marie quickly saw, the
clubs were important expressions of the power of the
Fairhope sisterhood.

From the moment Carrie Sykes met her in Mobile,
Marie was warmly accepted by the Fairhopers and soon
she became a major figure in the community. Not long
after she arrived my grandfather invited her to become
the associate editor of the *Courier* and to publish in it
extracts from the letters she wrote to her friends in
many parts of the world. In this way Marie became Fairhope's ambassador, explaining and interpreting its history to outsiders. At the same time she held up a mirror
in which Fairhopers might see themselves more clearly.
She plunged into many other activities as well, teaching
piano by the Chevé system she had written about a
quarter-century earlier, offering French lessons, and
translating occasional French works into English.

She also brought to Fairhope Edward's remarkable
book collection. They had taken over a thousand volumes with them to Mexico and now, after a period of
storage in Kansas, these were shipped to Fairhope to
become the nucleus of Fairhope's unique public library.
Early in 1900 she wrote of her books arriving, weighing
over eleven hundred pounds, according to the bill of
lading. Some were damaged, but she felt good having
them with her again. "I have put new stitches in the
rheumatic back of Julius Caesar; pasted the ragged clothing on the body of Juvenal, and straightened out the
folds and wrinkles in the face of many an old favorite,"
she wrote. Joseph Fels, Fairhope's wealthy benefactor,

looked over the catalog Marie sent him and wrote to
Grandfather that many of the books were "considerably
more ambitious than usual for a colony library." It is easy
to understand why he was impressed. Even today, when
the collection has been reduced to perhaps a third of its
original size, the volumes excite the intellect and imagination. Edward favored works of political theory and
philosophy, and of social criticism, but—good collector
that he was—he had also assembled fine first editions as
well as handsome printings of Shakespeare, Milton, and
other classics. The oldest volume was a Bible printed in
1611. Not surprisingly, the colonists persuaded Marie to
become the librarian. Fels made a handsome contribution toward a library building, even though he thought
the Howland collection "more ambitious than usual,"
and Marie saw to it that new books were added and that
reform journals were amply represented. The library
became an important center of colony activity, a continuing base for reflection and debate.[77]

-»>>X«<-

The women of Fairhope Marie came to admire and feel
comfortable with were zealous champions of political
equality who shared with Fairhope men the pleasures
and responsibilities of creating a new community. In
this respect they were radicals and they thought of
themselves as pioneers of a new social order. In other
respects, however, they were conventional, unlike the
sisterhoods Marie had first known in New York and
later celebrated in her novel and her advocacy of
Godin's social palace. Most important, Fairhope women
did not question the nuclear family, they accepted their
roles as mothers and homemakers, and the free-love
doctrines that had become part of Marie's own world

view were generally absent from their agendas. On the other hand, their confidence and their tolerance—in contrast to the women of Topolobampo—made it easy for them to accept and appreciate the occasional maverick who did come along, a fact that in time became one of Fairhope's main strengths.

Fairhope women, as Lynda Morgan writes, were "social feminists." They looked on the world as a "large home" and upon themselves as "social housekeepers." They accepted conventional sex roles—men as breadwinners, women as homemakers—while they stressed the special characteristics of women they believed would make the world a better place in which to live. Thus, they put special emphasis on the franchise because they believed it would free women not only to develop their own potentials but also because they had unique gifts to offer.[78] Marie, in fact, shared this view and expressed it as well as any of Fairhope's social feminists. The barbarity of war, for example, would give way to arbitration, she believed, if "women were free to exercise their powers—powers which untrammeled by false training would always make for peace and order." This was so, she wrote, not because the female was superior to the male, but because "nature has made her a passionate lover of beauty and order, the natural police of the world."[79]

For all their conventional attitudes toward sex roles— and notwithstanding the fact that the council had outlawed nude bathing from the association beach before Marie arrived (but not with her arrival in mind!)—Fairhope women were tolerant and open to advanced ideas about diet, dress, and idiosyncratic life styles.[80] There was a special receptivity among them to the idea that the wholesome development of the body was as important as the nurturing of the intellect. This was pleasing to

Marie because it echoed some of her theories of integral education; it also was a rich seedbed for Marietta Johnson's revolutionary educational experiment in organic education that started in 1907 and came eventually to reshape the Fairhope experiment. It was a spirit, too, that informed the discussion over dancing that gave Marie something of a fright when she first arrived.

Dancing had been one of her several problems in Topolobampo. A few months after she arrived in Fairhope, one of the association members raised a question at the Sunday discussion meeting about the morality of dancing and teaching children to dance. Marie boiled over in her column: "I most sincerely hope we shall discuss the question seriously and without ignorance or prejudice, until we find out that sin is not of the body, but of the soul." This was a battle she won. In fact, there was no real battle, for most of the Fairhopers shared her view, and a little later we find her describing one of the regular dances at the Fairhope Hotel where young and old together were enjoying each other's company. Dancing was not only good for one's physical development, Marie wrote. There was no better way to "stimulate more certainly and rapidly the noble and fraternal sentiments than by dancing with our brothers and sisters," she proclaimed, echoing in good Fourierist fashion the doctrine that dance symbolized cooperation in the state of Harmony.[81] Many times in the future she would note with pleasure how dancing, like music, brought Fairhopers together and helped them to forge bonds of community.

Happy in their attitude toward dancing, and gratified by the spirit and vigor of the Fairhope women, Marie found Fairhope a congenial place in which to continue her work in the woman's movement. With my grandfather's encouragement and support she saw that the *Courier* became a journal of advocacy and information, incorporating women's rights in the larger crusade for the single tax. She reported regularly on books and magazines coming into the library (and she helped to see that the flow of works on women was steady), urging Fairhopers to keep informed. Her sharp judgments were offered on a wide variety of topics—ranging from militant suffragism in Britain to women's property rights in Alabama—and she frequently reminisced about women (and men) who had been pioneers in the women's movement. When she corresponded with some of her old friends, she let Fairhopers know what they were currently up to. Victoria Woodhull, for example, was married and living in England but still working for the liberation of women and children. Closer to home, Marie used Fairhope examples to argue for sensible dress and freedom from restrictive conventions. Thus she wrote admiringly of a friend who wore "walking shorts" when taking "active exercise" and urged Fairhope women to do likewise. She could not understand why so many women wore dresses that necessitated "progress about as graceful as that of a rheumatic camel." On other occasions her strictures on dress were more political. When her friend Alice Herring spoke at the Progressive League wearing a hat, as she always did, Marie objected: "Why should we not bare the head when addressing audiences, since we require it of men?" Finally, she kept reminding Fairhopers of her own long-standing personal commitment. Writing of her membership in the American Woman's League she declared: "I could not see a great movement for woman's progress and not try to be in it. I have long known that the cause of woman is the cause of the world."[82]

As reference librarian, interpreter, elder stateswoman, and gadfly of the woman's movement, Marie made an inestimable contribution to the shaping of Fair-

hopers' thoughts about their experiment and its relationship to the larger social order they were hoping to
change. And it was happy work for her because she
aroused none of the hostility from other women she had
experienced in Topolobampo but, instead, found a
large community of women who admired and looked to
her for guidance. The children would remember her,
too. One who knew her has a vivid memory of the days
she spent in the library and of the impact Marie Howland had on her. She remembers that Mrs. Howland
stood for women's rights, and she did, too. Asked what
it meant—being for women's rights—she replied, "We
were just kids, teenagers, but we knew: it meant you
should always speak up when you had something to say
and you shouldn't be barred from anything because you
were a woman."[83]

Gratified by her role in the community, Marie found
herself shifting some of her previous feminist beliefs
even as she kept the main issues alive in her *Courier*
columns. Since the 1850s she had maintained that
women's liberation must rest on the foundation of their
economic independence. Fairhope's social feminists,
adamant about the right to vote, placed a lower priority
on this goal. Women were never barred from employment in Fairhope, and many became wage earners and
professionals. According to the 1900 manuscript census, nine of thirty-three adult women in the community
were employed. Eighteen of the twenty-two who were
not employed had children living at home. Fairhope
women took pride in the achievements of their sisters
who held jobs in the community (and who became important role models for future Fairhope women), but
the principal emphasis of their thought was on woman
in the home. That was where her chief contribution was
to be made.

Marie adapted to this climate of opinion. She continued to write occasional pieces arguing that women's economic dependence on men was the root of their subor-
dination to them, but more often she shifted to other
aspects of the woman's movement and, at the same time,
wrote that the woman's movement was part of a larger
crusade for equal rights. She herself, of course, was in
an anomalous position. An author, journalist, creative
librarian—a woman of independent spirit and many
talents—she was nonetheless dependent for her living
on the benevolence of two men: her first husband, Lyman Case, who had left a bequest for her in 1892, and,
later, Fiske Warren, a wealthy northern single-taxer and
Fairhope benefactor.

Other planks in her earlier feminist platform were
likewise modified or abandoned. She never appears to
have advocated cooperative nurseries either to make
possible employment for mothers or to facilitate integral
education for the children. Her columns brimmed with
praise of the children of Fairhope, and in Marietta Johnson—whose mission is the subject of the next chapter—
she found an educational philosopher whose practical
demonstration of organic education gave her new hope,
validated many of her old views, but did not transform
the conventional home structure. Nor did she seek to
bring relief to the homemaker by asking Fairhopers to
draw up plans for kitchenless homes. She wrote as forcibly as ever about "relentless, eternal" housework; about
the "eternal toil" that was "wearing" to the homemaker,
"damaging to good looks" and "hurtful to the nobler
self." But as a solution she proposed a modest alteration
of the family regimen, "some arrangement" whereby the
housewife "could always count on one day of compara-
tive rest." One refugee from the Ruskin socialist colony
started an "Economic Living Club," a cooperative dining

program for six households, but it served widows only and never evolved into a scheme for domestic revolution, grand or otherwise.[84]

Marie's shift away from her earlier notions of a grand domestic revolution was facilitated by her powerful commitment to Fairhope and its faith that women's liberation was not an independent variable or primary force in social change but, rather, a major goal that would be achieved as a consequence of remaking the entire social order. It was a powerful faith, a belief that the cooperative commonwealth based on the single tax would make all disparate elements fall into place. She was certain of her ground, though. Once she listened to a speaker at the Progressive League declare that the Socialist party was the first political party to make women's rights one of the planks in its platform. Professor Bellangee challenged this, saying that the Populist party had such a plank—he knew, because he had helped to draw it up. All the while Marie said she was reflecting on the relationship between the single-tax movement and women's rights, or what she preferred to call equal rights. Here the single tax won hands down, outranking "all organizations in the breadth and depth of its advocacy of equal rights."[85]

Her conversion to the Henry George doctrine seems to have been complete. Before she came to Fairhope she had little to say about George's ideas, although she must have been familiar with them. Edward certainly was and he was not impressed. He once classified Georgism "among the 'illusions' of which there have been so many in every department of 'civilization.' " He agreed that land must be common property, but saw that as little reason to become a single-taxer. Marie reasoned differently. For one thing, her bruising experiences at Topolobampo persuaded her that no rights of any sort were safe where there was not a deep commitment to individual rights. Too much "cooperation" and too little "individualism" was a dangerous thing. Most of the cooperative colonies, she believed, had come to early and bitter failure precisely for that reason. In Fairhope she said she thrilled at becoming "a worker for the cause I knew could not fail," and she put down as one of the main reasons for her confidence in success the fact that "the obligatory cooperation common to most socialistic associations has no existence here, yet the members are truly cooperative in spirit." This was precisely the point my grandfather argued regularly as he worked his way through the thicket of competing ideologies. To an English friend of Marie's he wrote that "under freedom," by which he meant under the single tax, "organized cooperation would naturally and voluntarily be resorted to in undertakings too large for individual capital and management," but otherwise the properly organized society would respect individual rights under the "law of equal freedom."[86]

Fairhope became for Marie an abiding and all-consuming cause. To a critic who complained that the Progressive League was too secular, that it rang in the single tax at every opportunity, she countered that "the fundamental principles of the Single Tax are consonant with, not creed, not ecclesiastical dogma, but with the very essence of religious faith." With such a faith, she found "life is worth living, if only for seeing the progress Henry George's philosophy is making all over the world." Everywhere she spread the good word—in the letters to her friends, in her columns, at club meetings and the incessant social gatherings—and when she visited the school her first concern was to learn how well the children were understanding their lessons in single-tax doctrine. There was a spirit about Fairhope, she believed, that swept all before it. Her close friend and frequent houseguest Alice Herring perhaps put it best. Writing from a Florida seaside resort, she recalled how Fairhopers disagreed on many subjects—usually vigorously—but were united on a fundamental principle for which they were willing "to make almost any personal sacrifice." There was a "spirit of comradeship" in Fairhope that Herring had never seen elsewhere. It gave meaning to life and direction to one's actions. "And so, in answer to your question," she wrote to Marie, "I must say I am lonely for the spirit of Fairhope, and I always am when away from there, even when at home; for no amount of personal love can take the place of the comradeship that unites a community. They are quite different, and one cannot supply the need of the other."[87]

Marie shifted the emphasis of her reform thought as a consequence of her commitment to Fairhope, but her numerous *Courier* essays on the subject show that she never lost her interest in Godin or her devotion to his social palace. Happily for her, Fairhope became—in its own special way—the Familistère she had longed for most of her life. She never made the connection directly, never proclaimed the creation of the "Fairhope Familistère," but it does not take too much imagination to make that connection now and to see in it the source of Marie's contentment with Fairhope and her sense of having fulfilled her destiny as a career reformer.

From the moment they acquired their first bay-front land, the colonists thought of how best to plan a physical environment that would be appropriate to their doctrine of "cooperative individualism." The site they chose, high on a bluff overlooking Mobile Bay, was uncommonly beautiful. Grandfather's first description of it came in a letter from one of the location committee members. "We viewed the land & country over the hills and along the shore," James Bellangee wrote. "It is lovely indeed. High banks and sandy beach with every here and there a spring gushing out of the bank. . . . The view from the shore is magnificent."[88] Grandfather was not disappointed. Shortly after arriving he wrote his own account of the site the Fairhopers chose:

> Here we have a short strip of sandy beach, then a narrow park . . . covered with almost every variety of shrub and tree which flourishes in this locality—pine, live oak, magnolia, cedar, juniper, cypress, gum, holly, bay, beech, youpon and myrtle. On the east of this "lower park," as we call it, a red clay bluff rises up almost perpendicularly to a height of nearly 40 feet. Along its serried edge tall, arrowy pines stand like sentinels looking out to sea. . . . From the top of the cliff, looking out above and between the lower rooted trees, the bay spreads in all its beauty.[89]

There was a natural knoll at the top of the cliff and one of the council's first actions was to reserve it, and all of the beach below, for the community. Creating this substantial park land was a signal that no individual was to monopolize scarce community resources, just as it demonstrated the colonists' belief that community development must be planned carefully and that places of special beauty and harmony must be set aside as communal gathering places.

Within the next few years cooperative efforts under council guidance involved most Fairhopers in the construction of their village. A road was cut down the steep hill leading to the bay; a wharf was built, and soon there was a community-owned boat, the *Fairhope*, to take persons and goods to Mobile and from there to the outside world. Village streets were laid out so that they widened as they approached the bay, and lots were terraced to give the maximum number of homes attractive views. A platform under a giant magnolia tree on the beach was a special gathering place—for serious discussions as well as frequent picnics—and it was soon supplemented by community-planned bathhouses on either side of the wharf. Cooperative planting efforts lined the main avenues with oaks and magnolias, a public well was dug, a water tower erected, a tasteful cemetery laid out, and before the end of the first decade a telephone system was operating. A private hotel went up near the bay as a lodging place for visitors and a gathering place for Saturday-night dancers. Public buildings included the schoolhouse, a hall for community meetings—the Progressive League met there when the weather forced it to move from the bluff—and a library next to Marie's home.[90] Marie was impressed by this record of cooperative community building, not only the physical accomplishments but also the ways in which Fairhopers had shared in the construction of their village—planning, debating, laboring, and celebrating with innumerable after-work picnics.

Within this cooperative framework Fairhope individualism flourished. Fairhopers chose lots and built homes and shops to suit their tastes and needs. For the use of the commonly owned land they paid rent to the community, but how they used the land was their decision, not the dictate of the community. Most of the plots were large enough for the colonists to have fruit trees and vegetable gardens and chickens and sometimes a cow or two. Many of them experienced the pride and intense satisfaction that comes from self-reliance and self-sufficiency—joys that had made Marie's Casa Tonti days so special to her. None was wealthy and there were no great disparities of wealth reflected in the homes and ways of life in the community. Satisfaction and a sense of achievement came from succeeding in one's own work, participating in the creation of a "model community," and knowing that the rare beauty of the bluffs, gullies, beaches, and bay belonged to everyone. Godin's social palace was designed to provide what he called the "equivalents of wealth"—the good things of life that were monopolized by a few, denied to the many. Fairhopers had a sense of possessing these "equivalents of wealth" without sacrificing their cherished individualism. It was a happy combination.

Marie, too, found happiness here, so that her natural optimism could flourish and overcome periods of pain and melancholy. She no longer grew many vegetables, but her flower garden was perhaps the finest in the community and she took great pleasure in it. She sometimes wrote as if all of Fairhope were a giant garden. "How glorious is Fairhope now with its gardens of roses," she wrote one April. "I venture to say there are more flowers in vases here, and more worn, than in any place of its size in the world." The variety was stunning: "The amaryllis, the Chinese primrose, the exquisitely fragrant Chinaberry tree, and hundreds of others . . . are nearly at perfection. The grancillium jasmines have long been in bloom and other jasmines and clematis are just opening." Next to flowers she wrote most about children. "Children and flowers!" she exclaimed: "As I look over my *Courier* file I find my contributions ablaze . . . with these subjects. I never tire of them." She was particularly fond of a child she called the Cherub, who made a regular path through her garden, but the town was "full of nice, pretty, respectful, polite children" who were a joy to her.[91]

A childless widow, Marie was not without family to share her old age. She was joined in Fairhope by the twin sisters whose care had fallen to her when their father died. All three of the New Hampshire Stevens girls—first Ada, then Marie, and finally Melissa—died in Fairhope.

The day after Marie died the Colony Council took special note, resolving that "in the death of Mrs. Marie Howland the Single Tax Corporation has lost one of its most loyal and valued members, to whom the Corporation and the community are deeply indebted." Perhaps thinking ahead to the hymn he would sing at her funeral, and mindful of the things that mattered most to both of them, my grandfather concluded the official notice of Mrs. Howland's passing with the proclamation that "hers was a life of useful activity devoted in unusual measure to unselfish effort for her fellow men and the world was better for her having lived in it."[92]

# The Mission of Marietta Johnson

THERE IS MAGIC IN MARIETTA JOHNSON'S NAME EVEN now, more than four decades after her death. Fairhope was a magnet for remarkable people, but none was as memorable as she. And no one who knew her is likely to have been untouched by the force of her overflowing personality and radical doctrines. My grandfather was the chief architect and principal leader of the community, but it was Mrs. Johnson who widened the scope and raised the sights of his experiment. Because of her it had a dimension and a destiny he did not dream of when he drew up the plans for his "model community"; and much of its fame radiated from what she created there. She and he were Fairhope's guiding spirits, dominating spokesmen for the new social order it was designed to demonstrate and hasten into being. When they died—he in 1937 and she in 1938—Fairhopers mourned their passing, sensing that the moorings of a lifetime had suddenly been washed away.

For Marie Howland, Fairhope was the climax of a long and brillant reform career, the place where she pulled together the rich and varied threads of her experience. For Marietta Johnson, Fairhope was the starting place, the launching pad for her brilliant reform career. When she arrived she was forming out of some newly acquired ideas the vision of a reconstructed world, but she had no plan of action, no reform agenda. Both she and her husband were socialists, but in the part of the country they came from that was not especially noteworthy. In fact, their lives were so unremarkable that—so far as anyone knows—neither of them was ever written about in the newspapers or magazines. Consequently, and in the absence of family memoirs, Marietta Johnson's history is the story of her Fairhope years. In Fairhope she made a palpable reality of her vision and from there she spread its hope and its fame. As she did she created such ferment that we are left with a richly documented record of her mission.

Marietta Louise Pierce and her twin sister were born in St. Paul, Minnesota, on October 8, 1864, two of the eight children of Clarence and Rhoda Martin Pierce. We know almost nothing about her childhood except for the recollections of relatives that the family was closely knit and deeply religious—the parents were among the founders of the First Christian Church of St. Paul—and that they lived for a while on a farm where the children sometimes saw Indians. Marietta's father died while she was a youngster and her mother ran a school in their home, teaching neighborhood children as well as her own. Marietta later attended the public schools of St. Paul and graduated from the State Normal School at St. Cloud in 1885. She was a successful teacher with a zeal for her profession that impressed her colleagues and won for her teaching positions in the normal schools of St. Paul, Moorhead, and Mankato. By the time she had reached her early thirties she was well established as a teacher of teachers. She and John Franklin Johnson—about whose youth virtually nothing is known—were married on June 6, 1897, while she was

teaching at Mankato, one of the best normal schools in
the area. Two years older than his bride—he was thirty-
four and she thirty-two when they were married—
Frank Johnson was from St. Paul. They lived in Mankato for a while after the wedding but moved in 1900 to
western North Dakota to make their home on a cattle
ranch. Their son Clifford Ernest was born there in the
spring of 1901.[1]

The young couple and their boy—remembered as a
bright, dark-eyed child—came to Fairhope during the
Christmas season of 1902. Marie Howland believed they
had been persuaded to come by Dr. Clara Atkinson, my
grandfather's half-sister, who was from the Twin Cities.
But there were several people from there with Fairhope
connections, including the Swift family, neighbors of
Dr. Atkinson in Fairhope. Both Frank and Marietta
were apparently looking for a change. His eyesight was
worsening and he had lung problems which they hoped
might clear up in a warmer climate. A niece wrote later
that Mrs. Johnson's health had been broken and that
she needed rest. Whatever problems she had must not
have been severe, however, because she plunged into
work almost immediately after she arrived, taking
charge of the colony school and giving it new zest and
leadership.[2]

A child in the Swift home was one of the first Fairhopers to come under the spell of the new teacher. Sev-
enty-five years later she recalled that Mrs. Johnson,
staying with the Swifts while Mr. Johnson was away
looking over prospects elsewhere, was a woman pos-
sessed. She has a vivid memory of how Mrs. Johnson,
every night after supper, would call out to Mrs. Swift:
"Em! Can you come up and put this baby to bed?" Mrs.
Swift always obliged and, with Clifford Ernest attended
to, Mrs. Johnson would "study 'til all hours of the morn-

ing, studying Dewey, Oppenheim, Henderson—they were almost her Bible."[3]

The book by Nathan Oppenheim, the attending children's physician at the Mount Sinai Hospital, was called *The Development of the Child*. It was published in 1898, but Marietta Johnson did not hear of it until 1901 when she returned to Minnesota to teach briefly at the St. Paul Teachers' Training School. Her superintendent handed it to her and recommended that she study it. It was a "scale dropper," she said of it later. "It clears the vision."[4]

In all of her accounts of this memorable episode, Mrs. Johnson insisted that her first feeling was one of dismay. She was an experienced teacher trained and seasoned in the best normal schools of Minnesota, proclaimed by the United States Commissioner of Education to be "among the best in the country." She was regarded as a success in her profession. To make matters worse for herself, she had wanted to be a teacher since she was a small girl. Now, after reading Oppenheim, she felt ashamed of the pride she had taken in her achievements, guilty about the praise she had received. Instead of boasting of the competence of her young pupils in reading and arithmetic, she was made to feel by Oppenheim that her conventional methods of teaching—no matter that her pupils could read and do sums—were "crippling children mentally, as definitely as physical ill-treatment would cripple them bodily." She looked upon herself as a "child destroyer." It was "then and there," when she finished reading Oppenheim, as she later told a *New York Times* reporter, that "I made up my mind that my own child . . . should never be put through the old, old mill. Mills crush. We do not want to crush the childish mind."[5]

Oppenheim preached a doctrine subversive of almost everything Marietta Johnson had learned from the established authorities of her day, and his claim that "the world has a wrong idea of its children" hit her with special force. Because of the false understanding of children and the force of their own needs and ambitions, parents and teachers required children to perform tasks for which they were not ready. Thus, kindness was all too often "turned to cruelty," Oppenheim wrote, and good "twisted into bad." Nor was the damage transitory. The harm done by conventional parenting and schooling, he wrote, "may extend over a whole lifetime." The "wrong idea" from which this destructive behavior arose was that children were in fact only small versions of adults whose main need was training in the acquisition and perfecting of skills and attitudes appropriate for adults. In elaborate detail Oppenheim attacked this popular assumption. The child "is in no way really like an adult," he argued, but "is absolutely different, . . . not only in size, but also in every element which goes to make up the final stage of maturity." The child's condition was one of "continuous change" that required "a special treatment and environment." For Oppenheim, therefore, the task of the teacher was to understand the true nature of childhood and then supply the appropriate nurturing environment for the child's wholesome growth. The child "is a creature of surrounding, modifying influence," he wrote, and is, "to a large extent, what his environment makes of him." Thus, "the responsibility for his development rests heavily upon those who provide the environment."[6]

Marietta Johnson underwent a conversion experience. Inspired by Oppenheim she formed a vision of herself as a teacher who would discover how to provide the right circumstances in which children might grow naturally, unforced and unwarped by external pressures. Without knowing it at the time, she was commit-

ting herself to the same faith in liberation through education that had stirred Rousseau, Pestalozzi, Froebel,
and other pioneers of child-centered education. Fortunately for her, her awakening came just at the moment
when America itself was aroused by a surge of progressive educational and social thought and she became an
eager student of each new innovative writer. C. Hanford Henderson, a prophet now long forgotten, and
John Dewey, the nation's preeminent philosopher of
the new education, were especially important to her,
both for their writings and their personal commitment
to her work. In Fairhope she found the ideal setting for
her vision to grow into a consuming thirty-year mission.
There she turned her unique distillation of progressive
thought into a one-person movement with radical messages calling for far-reaching social reconstruction.⁷

Marietta Johnson took over the public school when it
opened in January of 1903, much to the good fortune
of the community, according to the *Courier*. From the
start she made a deep impression on the Fairhopers.
Marie Howland, totally captivated by her new friend
and comrade, reported a few months later that Mrs.
Johnson was liked and admired by everyone, that she
was a "great worker" who had the remarkable power to
"awaken the spirit of study in her pupils," and that good
order prevailed in her school in easy harmony with
happy, unfettered movement of the children. This was
no ordinary educator, Marie told her readers. She understood Froebel and was, in fact, extending his kindergarten principles throughout the school. Fairhope was
fortunate to have so dynamic a representative of the
most "advanced thought" adding her efforts to the col-

community talent were reflected in the new departure. On New Year's Day, 1904, when the colonists held their annual celebration of the founding of the colony, Mrs. Johnson read a paper on "Education at Fairhope" in which she surveyed the changes that had taken place in the twelve months since her arrival and gave notice that the "new education" was sure to become one of the "good theories" Fairhope existed to demonstrate, meshing harmoniously with the single tax and public ownership of utilities as an essential ingredient in the commonwealth of cooperative individualism.[10]

On the day she spoke so hopefully about the future, the *Courier* carried the disturbing news that Frank Johnson had determined to take the family away from Fairhope. He had found a place in Mississippi where he thought "the conditions are better . . . for stock raising in which he intends to engage," the paper reported. Readers were promised that "Mrs. Johnson will at least remain in Fairhope until the close of the school year," but, in fact, she left in early April to join her husband in Barnet, Mississippi, a small town in Lauderdale County, whence Nancy Lewis had come over three decades earlier. There they bought a pecan farm, instead of raising stock, dropped for the time being the idea of a school, and added to the family a second son, Franklin, born in the spring of 1905. It was a "sad thought," Marie wrote when classes began in 1904 without her, "that we could not have Mrs. Johnson in permanent charge of our school."[11]

The Mississippi interlude was not a happy one for either Marietta or Frank. Early in 1905 their home burned. They rebuilt, but pecan farming never proved successful and Frank struggled with worsening eyesight, so that his wife had to do all the correspondence for him. She kept closely in touch with Fairhope and obvi-

ously longed to be back there. A few Fairhope children
came to live—and study—with her; she read the *Courier*
regularly; and she kept up a lively correspondence with
several Fairhope friends.[12]

Two friends who would come to have special influence
in her life were Samuel H. and Lydia J. Newcomb Comings. They had come to Fairhope at about the same time
as the Johnsons and shared many of Marietta's educational beliefs. Mr. Comings had written a book on industrial education, and Mrs. Comings was an authority on
physical culture. They were looking for the chance to
sponsor a school combining industrial education with detailed attention to nutrition and physical development.
During the winter of 1903–1904 Mrs. Johnson regularly
took her midday meal with the Comingses, who came to
admire her vision and to have great faith in her ability to
translate it into reality. Like other Fairhopers, they regretted her departure in 1904. Part of the disappointment was eased when they brought her back for a special
summer teachers' institute in 1906, under the auspices of
the George Academy. Mrs. Johnson conducted a demonstration kindergarten with local children and gave a series of lectures on child study and psychology. Marie
Howland, dazzled as ever by the magic of her friend
Marietta, visited the kindergarten and reported glow-
ingly on happy children intently absorbed in the story of
Hiawatha, showing how they could "imitate the voices of
the birds, the wind in the pines, and the rushing waters."
This was "real education," Marie believed, and the children would benefit from it the rest of their lives. Three-
quarters of a century later one who did made the same
judgment, recounting vividly her memory of that kindergarten. "It was a supreme delight," she told me with
sparkling eyes, "and I've remembered it all these years
with joy."[13]

During the summer of 1906 Fairhopers learned the name Mrs. Johnson gave to her theory of education. She called it "organic training" or "organic education" and, according to Marie, it was "the kindergarten method carried through the entire school course" just as "Froebel intended it to be." Mrs. Johnson borrowed the term "organic" from C. Hanford Henderson, whose book *Education and the Larger Life* had by this time become as important to her as Oppenheim's *The Development of the Child.* Both were required reading for students in the 1906 summer institute.

By "organic education" Mrs. Johnson meant that "education is growth," a definition John Dewey was to emphasize and plant firmly in the lexicon of progressive educators. When she said "education is growth," she meant that schooling should not be training or preparation for future demands but the proper nurturing of immediate needs of the whole organism. She called her idea "organic" education because she believed strongly that no part of a child's development could be isolated from another without the danger of warping the child. The spiritual, mental, and physical must always be kept in balance, she argued; stressing one to the detriment of another would damage the whole child. Henderson, in his chapter entitled "Organic Education," wrote of a "process of organic culture" which he defined as "the thoroughgoing culture of all sides of a man's nature," the process by which "he can come into a totality of power, and can satisfy that impulse toward perfection which is the most abiding impulse of the human spirit."[14]

As Mrs. Johnson worked out the details and pondered the implications of her theory of organic education, her ardor for Fairhope as the place where she should conduct a grand experiment intensified. In-

creasingly she came to see how the single tax and organic education were complementary, reinforcing reforms. Fairhope, moreover, was a community built on
the idea that American society must be shaken up,
wrested from its old fetters, and given new direction.
No more congenial setting for her work could be im-
agined and she must therefore have found the Mississippi exile something of a trial.

In a long letter to my grandfather, which he liked so
much that he published it in the *Courier*, Mrs. Johnson
wrote of the ways in which she saw Fairhope as the
antidote to the ills of the existing social order. Indicting
the Christian churches for the ways in which they
draped the mantle of righteousness over the "unjust
and un-Christian system" by which men were forced to
live, she likened them to the "animal breeder" who
hoped to "raise fine animals by denying them every condition of food and shelter necessary to their growth."
When "the very existence of the body depends upon
unrighteous dealing," she wrote, one could hardly expect a flourishing spiritual life, the emergence of real
Christianity. In contrast, she believed that the Fairhopers were engaged in "a greater Christian work than
that of any other organization of which I know" for they
were "seeking to establish conditions which make it possible for men to be Christians." Unlike the churches, she
wrote, Fairhopers went to the root of things, just as she
hoped she might do with an organic school. She ended
with an affectionate, wistful flourish: "We all read the
*Courier* regularly . . . and I live in Fairhope a great deal
of the time, although my physical being is up here in the
woods! . . . I am more interested than ever before in the
reforms for which Fairhope exists, and I should be
more than happy to be able to spend the rest of my life
in helping ever so little in so great a cause."[15]

Fortunately for her, Mrs. Johnson's good friends, the Comingses, felt the same way about Fairhope. Mr. Comings had written in the *Courier* of the "lofty ideal of human betterment" for which the colony stood and of the ways in which it was permeated with optimism and a passion for democracy. Yet Fairhope lacked a progressive school and a philosophy of child-rearing appropriate to its larger vision of social reconstruction. When Mrs. Johnson wrote to the Comingses in the summer of 1907 to tell them that life was unsatisfactory in Mississippi, that they must make a change, but that they had no definite plans, Mrs. Comings urged upon her husband a plan of action: "We have talked a great deal, now let's do something," she said. "Let's ask Mrs. Johnson to return to Fairhope and open a kindergarten . . . and make it financially possible for her to do it; . . . this will give her an opportunity to work out some of the problems which so interest us."[16]

In a small cottage provided by the Comingses and with a monthly stipend from them of $25, Marietta Johnson started her School of Organic Education in November of 1907. C. Hanford Henderson came down to celebrate the occasion and joined Mrs. Johnson in addressing the Progressive League on the promise of organic education. There were six local children in the kindergarten when it opened; a few older children, some from out of town, were also included in the new school. Marie was delighted with the prospects and overjoyed at having her friend back in Fairhope. "Every morning," she reported, Mrs. Johnson could be "seen by the roadside before her cottage, exercising with her pupils in running, jumping, etc." The school had hardly begun, however, when little Franklin, the Johnsons' younger son, died from a fall, a freak accident. Stunned by the loss of her child, Mrs. Johnson was hit with still another blow when her benefactor, Mr. Comings, suffered a fatal stroke on Christmas Eve.[17]

"We passed through deep waters," Mrs. Comings later wrote, recalling the weeks after the deaths of Franklin and her husband. For Mrs. Johnson, work was the best antidote, and after the Christmas holiday friends remarked on the appearance of her old zest. There was much to keep her busy. By the end of January there were twenty youngsters in the kindergarten and over thirty in the school. In February the Colony Council made the first $25 monthly appropriation for Mrs. Johnson's free kindergarten, thus formally launching a long and intimate association between the single-taxers and the Organic School. Additional building plans were announced soon, along with the news that Frank Johnson, who had turned down offers to teach elsewhere, would construct a shop in which he would offer instruction in manual training for the children of his wife's school. Abandoning plans for life on a farm, he spent his remaining years as his wife's shop teacher and faithful supporter.[18]

"The Organic School has proven its right to a place among the permanent things of Fairhope," my grandfather wrote at the end of 1908. Halfway through its second year, the school now had over fifty students. It was free to local residents, and tuition-paying students from the North were vigorously recruited with the promise that Fairhope was "one of the most desirable places in the south for people with children in which to spend the winter." Mrs. Johnson's plan for turning Fairhope into an educational laboratory, abandoned in 1904 when she moved to Mississippi, now seemed certain to be given a chance. Prospects were brightened notably by the announcement at the colony anniversary celebration on New Year's Day, 1909, that Joseph Fels had made a $10,000 contribution to the school.[19]

From the beginning Fairhope had a public school, probably the best in the county because the colony provided supplementary funds and attracted talented teachers. Now there would be two schools in a village of 466 white persons, 89 of whom were of school age.[20] Why should so small a community support two schools? Why did Marietta Johnson prefer a private school over the public one she had once managed and molded so well?

Mrs. Johnson knew that the colony influence gave the public school more maneuvering room than most such institutions had. On the other hand, it was subject to state regulations and popular assumptions—both of which were hostile to the fundamental precepts of organic education. Thus, the support she was offered from the Comingses, the colony, and Joseph Fels gave her the freedom to make the school precisely what she wanted it to be, without interference from anyone. At the same time, she was determined that hers would not be an ordinary private school—not even an ordinary private progressive school—conducted as a haven for those with incomes to pay high tuition fees. From the outset she ran her school as a model of what a public school should be, free and welcoming to all members of Fairhope, charging tuition only to the northern visitors.

For the colony, support of the school came early, but it was Mrs. Johnson who provided the rationale for the alliance, eventually weaving organic education so tightly into the fabric of the Fairhope design for a better world that visitors and Fairhopers alike thought of organic education and the single tax as two complementary ex-

pressions of the same urge for freedom and social democracy. Until Mrs. Johnson joined their ranks the Fairhopers, like Henry George himself, held no novel ideas
about education. They apparently assumed that the commonwealth of cooperative individualism to which they
were committed could be established and maintained
without modification of the competitive, individualistic
assumptions of the American school, so little were they
aware that the very system they wanted to change both
created and was sustained by those assumptions. Unlike
many of the communitarian experiments that had pre-
ceded theirs—one thinks especially of the stress Robert
Owen and Charles Fourier placed on cooperative, innovative child-rearing practices—the early Fairhope colonists put their faith almost exclusively in changing property arrangements, specifically in making land common
property and in socializing public services and utilities.
Mrs. Johnson also championed these reforms, but she
doubted their sufficiency. In one of her many Fairhope
speeches she put it this way: "No great economic reform
can be effected by people who have been trained during
the growing years to believe that success is in 'passing' at
school and in 'making money' in . . . life." The "first false
concepts of justice are formed in our schools," she said;
organic education would see that those "first false concepts" never took root and that children, experiencing
justice in their everyday lives, would "form a correct
concept of its meaning."[21]

As a prophet of social change through organic education, Marietta Johnson turned more to Dewey than to
Oppenheim or Henderson. By the time she started her
school Dewey was emerging as the most influential
American advocate of progressive education as the key
to social reconstruction. American schools, he wrote,
were "based on a conception of society which no longer

fits the facts—an every-man-for himself society," a cut-
throat, competitive society in which individualism ran
rampant over cooperation. He believed that class lines
were hardening and that economic exploitation was
bearing heavier on increasing numbers of citizens. He
wished for a new kind of school, not one that would
sanction and fortify these antidemocratic characteristics
but one that would become an embryonic community
foreshadowing the restructured society of the future, a
school community that would itself become an agent of
social change, a positive force in the creation of a new
democratic society.[22] This was the vision that stirred
Marietta Johnson, and it was her tenacious pursuit of it
that bound the school and the colony together in a common mission.

Dewey was an inspiration to Mrs. Johnson from the
beginning, but he did not visit her school until 1913, six
years after it had opened. Then he came at the request
of a newly formed organization hoping to spread Mrs.
Johnson's fame and influence beyond the borders of
Fairhope. Much had happened at the Organic School
between 1907 and 1913 to make this appeal to the famous Professor Dewey seem reasonable and for him to
accept it. Each year the school opened with more students and always the enrollment swelled in the winter
months with the children of northern visitors. Upton
Sinclair, who brought his son David to Fairhope to attend the school in 1909, was the first of a small number
of authors, intellectuals, and artists to discover Fairhope
through Mrs. Johnson. Along with the northerners,
two-thirds of all the local children attended, so that by
1913 there were as many as 150 pupils enrolled. The
teachers' training course drew local as well as nonresi-
dent converts. Long since too large for the small cottage
in which it had begun, the school now occupied a lovely

ten-acre campus, supplied rent-free by the colony, and boasted of several handsome, airy buildings. The Fels money was almost gone, but Mrs. Johnson was by now a strikingly successful fund raiser. Visitors to the school and the community helped by spreading the word of Fairhope's charms. One from Illinois wrote of the men and women "of strong individuality and positive ideas" who made up Fairhope and ended his essay demanding that the citizens of his home in Rockford send a delegation to the Organic School to see the perfect model for reconstructing their public school system.[23]

Meanwhile, Mrs. Johnson had begun her long forays into the North and Midwest, talking about Fairhope and about organic education, and in the process building a network of converts. Developing contacts through women's clubs, single-tax groups, civic organizations, and educational associations, she spent every summer from 1910 onwards on the lecture circuit. In 1911 she conducted a demonstration school at the University of Pennsylvania (working successfully with "problem children," *Courier* readers were told) before setting off for engagements in New Jersey, New York City, and the Midwest. By 1913 she was founding local organic school societies in both the East and the Midwest. In March of that year the *New York Times* published a full-page interview, presenting her ideas sympathetically and enthusiastically. A few months later she was lured to Greenwich, Connecticut, for what turned out to be the start of a major new chapter in her life.[24]

On one of her northern trips Mrs. Johnson met W. J. Hoggson, of Greenwich and New York City. They were traveling on the same train and fell into easy conversation about her mission. He seemed sympathetic and generous—Mrs. Johnson later wrote of him that "he made me believe for the first time in my life that it is possible for a businessman to be a Christian"—and a lasting friendship was formed. Hoggson introduced her to Mrs. Charles D. Lanier—May Lanier—of Greenwich. At Mrs. Lanier's home, where she was summoned for an interview and introductions to progressively minded women of the social elite, she learned of their interest in the new education. Calling themselves the United Workers of Greenwich, they were fascinated by what was happening in Fairhope and they persuaded Mrs. Johnson to conduct a demonstration school in Greenwich during the summer of 1913.[25]

"An experiment of unusual interest to mothers is being made this summer at Greenwich," the *New York Times* reported. "A woman of quite remarkable personality has been brought from a little Southern town and asked to try out her ideas in this community of rich New York suburbanites."[26] In the long *Times* interview of the previous March, which must have served for many of the women as their introduction to Mrs. Johnson's ideas, the Fairhope educator spoke of her social goals, stressing the ways in which she saw organic education as the enemy of hierarchy and special privilege. What appealed most to her Greenwich hosts, however, were the prospects of children growing up happy, well adjusted, self-disciplined, self-motivated, enjoying learning for its own sake. It is less likely that they took very seriously her doctrine that the intertwined economic and educational systems were built on injustice, breeders of vice and misery. For Mrs. Johnson organic education's ultimate aim was to nurture youngsters who, as adults, would recognize injustice and do something about it. The women of Greenwich, like so many other wealthy converts to progressive education, had a tendency to look upon the new education as another special privilege for their already privileged children.

Marietta Johnson managed to balance this paradox
with relative ease. She was an enormously self-confident
woman, easy and open in her personal relations, and
always optimistic. Thus, she found the Greenwich
workers agreeable allies. Of course, she needed the
help—and the money—they seemed able to give her.
Mrs. Lanier had a small school on her estate and she
urged Mrs. Johnson to leave Fairhope to direct it. "I
could never feel quite willing to do this," she wrote later,
explaining her decision to make Fairhope her permanent home and base of operations. "The simple environment of Fairhope, and the fact of charging no tuition from the people of the vicinity, gave a freedom to
work out an idea which could not be approached in the
more sophisticated community, though I hoped to be
able to work out the principle in the more complex environment and fully believed this to be quite possible."[27]
Instead of moving to Greenwich, Mrs. Johnson made it
the northern base of her Fairhope movement. At the
end of the 1913 summer school her friends there established the Fairhope League. Renamed the Fairhope
Educational Foundation in 1920, it raised money for the
Fairhope school, helped coordinate Mrs. Johnson's increasingly active lecture schedule, assisted her in founding satellite schools in various parts of the country, and
for over two decades sponsored the Fairhope Summer
School, attracting to Greenwich teachers, parents, social
workers, and others eager to meet Marietta Johnson
and to learn about organic education.

During the third Greenwich summer session a *New Republic* editor came out to have a look. He reported that
"Professor Dewey's dictum that the child can only be

educated by concerning himself with what has meaning to him as a child, and not what is to have meaning to him later as an adult" was better understood and applied by Marietta Johnson than by anyone in America. Learning under her guidance, he believed, "becomes as natural as eating." By the time this glowing assessment appeared the famous Professor Dewey had already visited Fairhope and published his evaluation of it. At the end of the 1913 summer session, the newly formed Fairhope League asked him to visit the Organic School. The idea appealed to him, but his schedule was tight: he could visit only during the Christmas holiday season. Mrs. Johnson discussed the importance of the visit with her pupils and they voted enthusiastically to come to school during their vacation period so that Dewey might see them. With these arrangements made Dewey came, bringing his fourteen-year-old son along with him. The youngster attended the school for the week they were there and liked it so much that he asked his father if he might remain for the rest of the year.[28]

The report Dewey made to the Greenwich organization was subsequently expanded and appeared in *Schools of Tomorrow*, a study of the leading experimental schools of the nation that Dewey wrote with his daughter Evelyn. He was as impressed by the Fairhope school as his son had been. It was a "decided success," he wrote, for it

demonstrated that it is possible for children to lead the same natural lives in school that they lead in good homes outside the school hours; to progress bodily, mentally, and morally in school without factitious pressure, rewards, examinations, grades, or promotions, while they acquire sufficient control of the conventional tools of learning and study of books—reading, writing, and figuring—to be able to use them independently.[29]

Natural, unselfconscious growth was the key, Dewey believed, and it sprang from Marietta Johnson's belief—

which Dewey traced back to Rousseau—that children grow most happily and successfully when what they experience has meaning for them as children. Dewey also sensed the depth of Mrs. Johnson's commitment. She believed, he wrote, that "the child has a right to enjoy his childhood," thus stressing her conviction that organic education was part of a revolution for human rights. Not surprisingly, then, Dewey found the school to be free from pressure. Children under eight or nine, for example, were not forced to read—and, consequently, they were bustling with activity and curiosity. Children followed the natural course of a good home where they moved from one interesting object to another, spontaneously in response to their own needs, learning about what they encountered and coming to understand relationships among the objects in their lives. One discovery led to another so that all skills were learned at the appropriate time, in satisfaction of the child's need, not in obedience to an adult's demand—although Dewey certainly saw Mrs. Johnson's strong shaping hand at work in all aspects of the school's management. The joy of learning which he observed—and which so charmed his son—was evident in the many school activities Dewey listed: "physical exercise, nature study, music, hand work, field geography, story telling, sense culture, fundamental conceptions of numbers, dramatizations and games." Much of the time was spent out-of-doors—an observation every Fairhope visitor made and one which Dewey's book captured best by a photograph of children working arithmetic problems on the banks of a gully. Handwork was especially stressed and Dewey was pleased to report that "boys and girls alike do cooking and carpentry work" where "the object . . . is not to train them for any trade or profession, but to train them to be capable, happy members of society."[30]

Comparing Organic School students with pupils in conventional schools, Dewey wrote that the Fairhope children were "apt to be stronger physically and are much more capable with their hands, while they have a real love of books and study that makes them equally strong on the purely cultural side of the work." Their "freedom from self-consciousness," he believed, unleashed initiative and enthusiasm and increased the pupil's "power to indulge his natural desire to learn, thus preserving joy in life and a confidence in himself which liberates all his energies for his work." The result of this happy and unique set of circumstances, Dewey concluded, was that the student "likes school and forgets that he is 'learning'; for learning comes unconsciously as a by-product of experiences which he recognizes as worth while on their own account."[31]

Dewey ended his study by returning to the theme of social reconstruction. To educate the "whole individual" was a revolutionary proposal with ramifying consequences for American society. "The democracy which proclaims equality of opportunity as its ideal requires an education in which learning and social application, ideas and practice, work and recognition of the meaning of what is done, are united from the beginning and for all," he wrote. Schools like the one in Fairhope, he believed, clearly showed "how the ideal of equal opportunity for all is to be transmuted into reality."[32]

It was a rave review that Mrs. Johnson and her friends in the Fairhope League put to good use many times in the years ahead. Dewey was an unrivaled authority and his unqualified and enthusiastic praise of the Organic School was precisely the stamp of approval Mrs. Johnson needed to confound skeptics, especially those whose credulity was strained by the claim that a progressive school, a model for America, was flowering in the Deep South.

Armed with Dewey's endorsement and continuing support, bolstered by the pride and approval of the Fairhopers, and kept solvent by a steady flow of northern pupils and the steadfast support of the Greenwich ladies and the Fairhope League, Marietta Johnson set out to convert the nation to what she grandly called "The Fairhope Idea in Education." She took charge of the Edgewood School in Greenwich and founded and staffed organic schools in Upper Montclair and West Orange, New Jersey, and in Indianapolis, Indiana. Her lectures took her to most parts of the country, although she did not penetrate the Far West until the late teens and twenties. *Courier* readers became accustomed to accounts of her "semi-annual flights to the north," one report noting twenty-three public addresses in twenty-six days. She was a charismatic personality, a powerful, persuasive speaker. The newsclips in the scrapbook of her speaking tours testify to her eloquence, and stories abound in Fairhope today—told by those who heard her speak—of her ability to sway huge audiences as well as arouse the ardor of intimate gatherings in parlors and classrooms.[33]

Encouraged by her support and success, sensing that progressive education was the wave of the future, and audacious enough to believe that her own vision of that future could become the vision of the nation, she approached Stanwood Cobb, an admirer, a zealous progressive educator, and an organizer with influence and ability. Would he endorse "The Fairhope Idea in Education" as the model for the progressive education movement in America? According to Patricia Graham, Cobb deflected her approach. "He was sympathetic with the Fairhope experiment," Graham writes, but "he doubted the wisdom of a national organization committed to a single educational philosophy." As an alternative, Mrs. Johnson suggested an organization that would study and publicize current educational experiments. Cobb found that proposal more agreeable. The result was the formation of the Progressive Education Association in 1919 with Cobb as the chief organizer. Marietta Johnson, one of the four speakers at the founding banquet in Washington, could take much of the credit for the formation of the new group. In her history of the association, Graham says that its creation was, for Mrs. Johnson, a dream come true. That may be so, but it was not her fondest dream, for that was of a national organization to promote the Fairhope idea, with the Organic School as the demonstration model and her at the center of the new movement.[34]

Mrs. Johnson was nearing the peak of her national fame when the Progressive Education Association was launched. Her school would reach its zenith in the 1920s. She had nearly two decades of work before her, both in Fairhope and in the nation. But she would have to manage without her husband during those years, for Frank Johnson died in Greenwich in the summer of 1919. He fell ill in Fairhope, Mrs. Johnson left the summer school to come home to be with him, and she took him back North where he soon died. By all accounts he was a supportive husband who managed well his role as "Marietta Johnson's husband." She was the successful one professionally, the one who sparkled and stood out in social circles. He had a tendency, one Fairhoper recalls, of drifting to the edges of the room while crowds gathered around his wife. But there appears to have been no resentment.[35]

One of Frank Johnson's former pupils in the manual training class complained to me that "they don't ever tell enough about him," and others remember him with special fondness. The shop must have been a good one.

Dewey said it was the best he had ever seen. "Usually, when the children are free," he explained, "the technique is not good, and when the technique is good the children are not free. Here, the technique is good and the children are free." More than a shop teacher, Johnson was a "true yokefellow in the building and conduct of the school," according to a friend who had known him in Mankato and Fairhope. Everyone remarked on how he kept up things at the house, where the regime was always simple, and on how he looked after Clifford Ernest when his wife was away on her speaking tours. In addition to his role as husband and collaborator, Frank Johnson played an important part in community life. He served on the Colony Council and in 1912 he was elected mayor. His widow was not quite fifty-five when he died. She had much energy left for her mission.[36]

In the spring of 1920 Marietta Johnson was in Washington for the first annual convention of the Progressive Education Association. The speech she made was the most radical the delegates heard. "The essence of the new education is to find out what is good for the child," she began. To do that, and then, acting on that knowledge, to provide the "right conditions of growth"—to "simply let the child *grow right*"—would guarantee a better quality of humanity, genuine progress of the human race. The nation would be transformed in a single generation.[37]

It was a soaring speech, claiming much for the new education and almost wholly lacking in subtlety and sophistication. A later speaker thanked Mrs. Johnson for the inspiration and example she provided. No one seems to have been untouched by her personal force, but others must have wondered how her own demonstration of the new education really worked. Her first questioner, for example, wanted to know how her students managed to enter college since they were assigned no grades and took no examinations. The question may have been a friendly one—there is no way from the convention proceedings to tell—but the claims made for the Organic School seemed to some of her friends then, as they have seemed to friends and critics alike in the years since her death, to need grounding in the palpable reality of the school.[38] What really went on in Fairhope? How did the grand process of making a better race actually work?

What actually went on in the school had been described many times by 1920 and by that year it had achieved a maturity so that its structure and curriculum were fairly well fixed, although innovative teachers, who came in considerable numbers during the 1920s, might always modify things. Children entered the school at age four, generally, for two years in the kindergarten. For the next six years they were grouped into three "life classes," with two age groups in each class, older children often helping younger ones. Then came two years of junior high school, followed by four years of high school.

Marietta Johnson often said that organic education was neither "a system nor a method," but "a point of view." It was a point of view that emerged from shared values and assumptions about childhood as well as about life. The world as it existed was artificial and warping because it denied children their right to natural growth. The organic point of view held that the right conditions for that growth would nurture a sincere and unselfconscious emotional life, stimulate intellectual inquiry as a natural expression of the desire to know, and respect the needs of a delicate nervous system. How these needs were to be met was a subject of considerable debate among progressive educators, but Marietta Johnson, although she denied having a "system" or a "method," had no doubt about what the main outlines of her school's requirements and expectations ought to be.[39]

Like most other progressive educators, Mrs. Johnson abolished the fixed desk, to give her pupils freedom of movement, simultaneously releasing tension and stimulating active, natural learning. She was less typical when she abolished all assignments for younger children. Set amounts of work for an entire group sprang from a misplaced faith in standardization, she remonstrated, claiming that standardization was "absolutely unnecessary" and "uneducational" as well. "Our children work because of the interest and according to their individual capacity," she explained, "and since every individual is unique there can be no other reasonable standard of accomplishment." A third departure from traditional education—and one she sometimes ranked as her most important—was the grouping of pupils by age, not academic ability, and the rigorous insistence that no child might fail. She prohibited all rewards, recognitions, and honors for "success" and likewise banned every form of punishment for "failure."[40]

It was not, as casual critics were then and are now likely to assume, a do-as-you-please school in which children, in unselfconscious and sincere bliss, followed caprice into confusion and chaos. On the contrary, as one of the early graduates puts it, "nothing could be further from the truth. . . . It was such a beautifully regulated school that you didn't have any feeling of discipline and that was because the children were so interested in what they were doing."[41] Mrs. Johnson, however vague she may have been about it in her writings, knew exactly what she thought was right and nurturing for children, and one of her gifts was her ability to communicate clearly to her teachers both her faith and her concrete expectations of them and their pupils.

One of those teachers, coming to Fairhope about 1920, later wrote of her teaching at the Organic School. "Fairhope was an ideal setting for this experiment," Lillian Rifkin wrote. "On the beach at Mobile Bay, the eight, nine and ten-year-olds built Indian tepees. We slept in the tepees and lived as Indians for a week. One of the mothers helped us prepare our meals which we cooked over an open fire. The children made beads from chinaberry seeds and dishes from the clay of the gully banks. Small [miniature] canoes were carved from the bark of trees and sailed into the bay." Such experiences were what Marietta Johnson would have called "the basics," had such a term been in vogue. Some years later, for example, she explained to an inquirer that "children should not be taught to read until eight or nine or ten years of age. . . . The children in our school under eight years of age have singing and dancing, a great deal of hand-work, stories, free play, and nature. We postpone the use of books entirely until eight, and then we do not require any degree of attainment or achievement for promotion."[42]

Mrs. Johnson banned the teaching of reading to six- and seven-year-olds (and sometimes to eight- and nine-year-olds as well) because she believed it strained the nervous system, inhibited clear thinking, and was likely to warp the child's social development. Lillian Rifkin, who taught the "second life" class of eight- and nine-year-olds, saw only good in such an approach. Her previously untutored students learned to read books in one week that first graders elsewhere "struggled with for months." Rifkin was approving of everything about the

Organic School. "There were no reports or exams," she learned. "No sense of worry, sleepless nights or tenseness was caused by examinations, nor did cheaters develop. . . . Each child was encouraged to express and develop his own interest according to his individual ability. He was not categorized as a smart or stupid child but was considered as a whole human being."[43]

Just as the concern for the "whole human being" did not result in a do-as-you-please school, without structure or discipline, so its students and teachers found it to be a place where there were clear and compelling standards. They were not the standards of a competitive social order, standards by which one could be measured and placed in a continuum in relationship to one's peers—those were the standards Mrs. Johnson fought to ban from American education. She herself often put it—maddeningly, perhaps, to some of her friends—that she simply expected all children to do their best, whatever that might be. No measure for such a standard has ever been invented, nor did Mrs. Johnson suggest one; but one has no doubt that she was a sure and fair judge of honest effort. Marietta Johnson was, of course, a standard herself. Her own expectations became a powerful force in the school, working on fellow teachers and students alike. Nearly every student of hers I have interviewed has remarked on what it meant in their lives to fulfill the expectations she had of them. There was "a standard there," one recalls; "it went very, very deep." This woman remembers asking herself frequently, "Would Mrs. Johnson approve of this?" Another recalled that "I was convinced that she expected me to do nothing improper and I wanted not to disappoint her." Still another, recalling a newcomer who said he would not work unless made to, remembers the shock; at Organic one worked because it was expected, the thing one did.[44]

These internalized values highlight the school's success in establishing standards and expectations that the students themselves believed were set in reference to them as individuals—respectful of their unique characteristics, needs, and potential. This was an especially important outcome for the high school program. Critics doubted then—as they have since—that a child-centered school, one totally free of rewards and punishments as incentives, could work where serious intellectual inquiry is at stake. According to the conventional view, hard work—because it is hard work—requires carrots and sticks and plenty of them. Marietta Johnson gave no quarter on this issue. Carrots and sticks were inherently harmful, miseducative, the sources of fear, insincerity, and hypocrisy. Hard work, moreover, was natural and inevitable when the student saw it as a matter of his own interest. Reaching that goal was not always easy for the school, she knew, but she was fiercely determined to pursue it. Over the years she replied to incredulous correspondents, setting them straight on her beliefs. Selections from her correspondence, better than anything else, suggest the depth of her commitment as well as the ways in which she could raise the hackles of the unbelieving:

> I am very happy to say that we do not have any report cards whatsoever. I am also delighted to say that we have no grades or standards for promotions and I am also pleased to tell you that we make no reports to parents either of scholarship or behavior. . . . We believe it is . . . destructive to the sincerity and unselfconsciousness of the child . . . to let him know that any report is being made of his work. We believe intellectual progress should be just as unselfconscious as his spiritual and physical progress.[45]

> I have found that parents are not usually to be trusted. They are much inclined to discuss reports with the children. This all makes for self-consciousness. We are very anxious that our children shall not

feel that the school is watching them and reporting upon their behavior or their progress, but that we are making every effort to provide conditions that they may have a happy life.[46]

We could not make a report on attainment in subject matter since many children would fail after the most earnest effort, which would be manifestly unfair. We could not make a report on attitudes, morals, or social relations since that would also develop most undesirable self-consciousness. . . . We feel that to grade children on intellectual attainment is unfair and undemocratic. We feel that grading children on morals may develop hypocrisy. We feel that it is absolutely impossible to grade children on spiritual or social development. So there we are. We have fallen back on the beautiful scripture, "Judge Not."[47]

Of course, the real outcomes of all education are spiritual and therefore unmeasurable. We rejoice from time to time at what we call the marked improvement or "coming out" of various pupils. This is not always indicated by unusual interest in school subjects, but in social adjustments, happiness, better health and general interests. We believe that education is growth and that the school program must minister to growth. This, of course, is impossible to really evaluate.[48]

With such a formidable protective barrier guarding their spontaneity and unselfconscious intellectual growth, students in her high school studied the same subjects—history, literature, ancient and modern languages, mathematics, and science—that made up the curriculum in conventional schools. The offerings at the Organic School were probably richer than those in the ordinary public school (especially in the foreign languages) and, of course, Mrs. Johnson's own course in the single tax was not duplicated elsewhere. For the most part, the academic curriculum at Fairhope was distinguished not so much by what the students studied, by the subject matter, as by the way they went about studying it. Freed from grades and the urgency of bringing students "up to standard," the teachers could more successfully nurture powers of analysis and expression. One of the history teachers drew modest national attention with an interesting four-year plan of historical study, but there was no tendency to slight traditional areas of intellectual concern in favor of "relevance" or idiosyncratic interests of particular teachers. The academic program was student-centered, flexible, and very lively—but within a framework of generally traditional subjects and authors.[49]

Judged by conventional standards, the students did well. They were admitted to more than a dozen colleges and universities without examination, solely on Mrs. Johnson's recommendation. Once in college, and sometimes after a period of adjustment to grades and examinations, they built on what one observer called "the freshness and sincerity of intellectual attack" they had learned in Fairhope. Another described them as "buoyant, well poised, free from either timidity or aggression" and believed that "those who have passed from this school into our universities have so far invariably proved their scholarship." Arthur Morgan, president of Antioch College, was pleased with those who had come to study there. "They have made the most of their native endowment," he wrote. "If you have more like them, send them along." One alumna, who was an intellectually gifted youngster, thinks that the students of her day tended to be admired more if they were well rounded and athletic than if they were brainy. Nonetheless, she recalls that academic work at the Organic School was as stimulating and fulfilling as any she had at the conventional schools she attended.[50]

Organic students did well by unconventional standards as well as by conventional ones. One observer wrote that "Fairhope graduates . . . acquit themselves creditably in colleges . . . and are splendid unspoiled human material besides." The lives of those students, she believed, would "argue powerfully" for Mrs. Johnson's educational theories. The "unspoiled human material"—the education of the "whole individual"—was, after all, the ultimate goal. Academic excellence was welcome, but it was not proof of success, either of the school or of the student. For the school curriculum this meant that woodworking, other crafts, and the arts— music, drama, and folk dancing—were continued through the high school years, ranking in importance with the academic subjects. They were never thought of as "extracurricular." In fact, in a discussion of the high school program Mrs. Johnson wrote that the shop was "the most important place on campus," and she frequently praised folk dancing as an ideal activity for people of all ages in the community and felt that it should be one of the few required courses in a proper college curriculum.[51]

Marietta Johnson valued these activities because they facilitated self-expression, nurtured the creative instinct, promoted poise and self-confidence, and generated a sense of well-being that spilled over into and enriched other areas of life. But she also valued them because they helped "socialize" the students, helped them to balance their innate individualism with community concerns and a cooperative spirit. With the academic courses she balanced individualism and cooperation by eliminating individual recitations, encouraging group discussions and team projects, asking students to share information and knowledge, and stressing mutual responsibility for attacking intellectual problems. With the creative handwork and the informal dramatic and musical productions she minimized the competitive urge and promoted wider concerns for the whole group.[52] She particularly favored folk dancing for the ways in which it developed physical skills within a context of changing partners, mutual dependence, and satisfaction in the achievements of the whole school. Her great success here was regularly symbolized by periodic school gatherings at which everyone danced—often with Mrs. Johnson "leading out" and parents, alumni, townspeople, and visitors alike joining in. Old English country, Morris, and sword dancing were introduced in the teens, and under Charles Rabold's leadership in the twenties English folk dancing became one of the school's most prominent identifying features.

There was little in the way of competitive athletics in the early years, and one suspects that if Mrs. Johnson could have had her way completely she would not have sanctioned them at all. But by the twenties the school had a football team and a baseball team for the boys and basketball teams for the boys and girls. Compromising here, she steered the passion for athletics into "organic" channels so that sports in the school were notable primarily for enjoyment of the game, lack of exclusion, team spirit, and the absence of a lust for victory. The 1924 school yearbook, for example, noted the winning record of the girls' basketball team but particularly celebrated their reputation for "sportsmanship"; the boys won the county championship, we learn, and "each player did his best and each deserves mention."[53]

In addition to the classes and the performances and the games, Organic School students were regularly involved in ad hoc independent activities that were an extension of the rich program Marietta Johnson designed for them. They helped to build classrooms. Comings Hall, the large auditorium, folk dance center, and community gathering place, was erected with student help and regularly repaired by students. They planted gardens and sometimes supplied the products for the

School Home dining room; they sewed uniforms for the baseball team; and they routinely tidied up their unique campus. "We did everything that was done," a former student recalls, "and we never had any criticism." Another remembers that she learned independence and self-reliance as she deepened her attachment to the school. Every student from the mid-twenties recalls the thirty-four-foot schooner that was built in the shop under the direction of history teacher Willard Edwards. The *Osprey* sailed in the bay for many years after it was launched in 1927, taking the folk dance team to Biloxi, high school students to the circus in Mobile, and faculty and students alike on numerous local outings and picnics.[54]

Students at the Organic School were an interesting and varied group. An April 1920 count reported 220 students enrolled, 72 of whom were from out of town, mostly from the North; 148—two-thirds of the total— were from Fairhope. Enrollment figures varied markedly during the next decade, sinking to a low on one occasion of just over a hundred to a high of upwards of two hundred. For most of the decade about half of the local children attended the Organic School, the other half going to the public school. Because it was free to local children, it attracted a good cross section of the population. "Mrs. Johnson maintained that you could run a school very successfully on any system whatsoever if you were careful about the children you took," one of the school's astute alumnae told me. The much-revered Dr. Henderson, she pointed out, went over his applicants "with a fine-tooth comb." With Mrs. Johnson it was the other way around: she insisted on having everybody.[55]

The proportion of local children to out-of-towners was generally more than two to one, but one of the distinctive—and decisive—facts about the school was the presence of the northerners. Many parents came to live in Fairhope for several months in the winter, bringing their young children to be in Mrs. Johnson's school. In 1921 a large School Home was opened on the campus. Mrs. Johnson moved into it—she lived there the rest of her life—along with the boarding students who paid for tuition as well as for their keep. The boarding students, some of whom came from prominent or well-to-do families, added money and a cosmopolitan touch to the school. The local children profited from the connection with the outside world, and the boarders were generally accepted into the Fairhope culture.

Among the boarders was generally a "backward" child or two, handicapped in one way or another. Mrs. Johnson always insisted that her school was not for "undeveloped" or "subnormal" or "backward" children, but her correspondence also reveals her tendency to make exceptions. She seems to have had a commitment to what we would call today "mainstreaming," at least on a modest scale. The disadvantaged would be helped by the school and the normal children had much to learn from those with handicaps. Of one such person an alumnus told me: "She made him the best citizen of the community that could have been made of him."[56]

The Organic School was an important turning point in the lives of many from afar who came to it for only brief periods, and it transformed for the better the lives of the local children who were in it for longer periods of time. Fairhope also was a turning point for many remarkable young teachers. Grace Rotzel, who came in 1921, later wrote: "I was astonished by the freedom and the openness. . . . I entered into teaching there with zest, delighted that I had to join all the creative work going on. . . . I stayed five years and, like many others, acquired the inspiration and confidence I needed for carrying on the ideas in subsequent teaching." Rotzel founded her own successful progressive school in Rose Valley, Pennsylvania, and when she wrote its history she remarked that she "became convinced of the need for change in education" in Fairhope, where she also gained "the confidence to work toward this end." Past eighty when I interviewed her at a retirement village, she lit up with memories of the Organic School. "Fairhope was a very unusual place," she told me. "You were lucky you were born there."[57]

Lillian Rifkin first met Marietta Johnson at the Greenwich summer school. Already a convert to Dewey, Rifkin said Mrs. Johnson "expressed everything I had ever felt about the education of the child." She went to Fairhope and after that to other progressive schools—the Modern School at Stelton, New Jersey, and then the Walden School in New York. When she came to write of her lifetime in progressive education, Marietta Johnson and John Dewey were two of the persons she recorded as having played a major role in her life. Like Rifkin, Sherwood Trask also taught at several progressive schools, including the Modern School where he was highly regarded before he came to Fairhope. From Fairhope he went to A. S. Neill's international school at Helleraue, near Dresden, and then to the Walden School. Wharton Esherick came to Fairhope in 1919, joined the Organic School faculty, met Sherwood Anderson, and "acquired his first set of carving tools." He later became America's preeminent furniture maker and woodworker. Paul Nichols, described by a Chicago-trained social psychologist as a sort of rural genius, met Mrs. Johnson in 1919 and was virtually commanded by her to leave what he was doing, bring his wife and children to Fairhope, and become second in command at her school. He remained there off and on for more than two decades. Charles Rabold was in the Yale music department when he came under Mrs. Johnson's spell. A disciple of Cecil Sharp, the English folk-dance authority, Rabold taught for Mrs. Johnson at both Greenwich and Fairhope. He was a "magnificent person," according to one of his pupils who remembers that "when Charles would enter the room with his great beautiful boisterous, outgoing way everybody would have to sing and everybody would have to dance." Even the most skeptical boys took to folk dancing under Rabold's guidance. He was Mrs. Johnson's assistant director and heir apparent when he was killed in an airplane accident in 1930.[58]

Marietta Johnson recruited lively, talented teachers who shared her vision and optimism. Some came after a summer with her in Greenwich; some were drawn by her national reputation; some were local women and men, graduates of her two-year teachers' training class. At one time or another there were graduates of Cambridge and Oxford as well as Harvard and Yale. They were an extraordinary group, but they were not enough to insure the educational revolution to which their leader was so fervently committed. Children were educated outside the classroom, away from the school campus—by parents, by their peers, by community leaders. Somehow all the significant figures in the child's life had to become part of the organic education experience, accepting its values and nurturing its institutions. "If right growth were understood and provided for," Mrs. Johnson told a Fairhope group, "we would have a better world in one generation."[59] To spread that understanding, she knew that she had to go beyond the school and into the community.

She had always been deeply involved in Fairhope affairs and had long since forged an intellectual alliance between the colony and the school. In 1921 she conducted a six weeks' winter course that would become a permanent part of her experiment and crusade. Her idea was to bring together parents, teachers, and social workers from various parts of the country to join Fairhopers in studying the school and its philosophy. "All adults form the environment of childhood," one notice explained; the purpose of the winter course was "to prepare adults to be the desirable companions of growing children." The *New York Times* made a similar point: "To be the fit environment of childhood, the Fairhope School . . . believes all adults should have special courses in school work." What Mrs. Johnson wanted was for adults actually to see and experience the things that had meaning for children—handwork, free play, nature walks, dancing, drama—as well as read Dewey and Oppenheim and Henderson and listen to her lectures. From the beginning the course was a huge success. Seventy persons attended the first year; in 1930 the *Courier* reported that winter course students had come from thirty-one states, Canada, and South Africa. Local attendance was likewise strong as the course became a major cultural event.[60]

For Fairhopers the winter course always meant a buzz of excitement. One woman, lamenting her presumed inability to get across to me "the interaction, the free-flowing feeling of the community and the school" explained that "all sorts of people came here: artists, Theosophists, philosophers, scientists, just marvelous people from north, south, east, and west." Not all of them came for the winter course, but most of the visitors did come in the winter, which was the time when Fairhopers reflected most seriously on their goals and values, and basked in the attention paid them by such regulars as Clarence Darrow, who spoke on how crime would be reduced if the single tax and organic education were to spread.[61]

Marietta Johnson's influence on young mothers and fathers must have been profound, because many of them consciously incorporated her teachings in their parenting. "She was the most fascinating lecturer I ever heard," one woman recalls, explaining to me that after she heard Mrs. Johnson lecture she would say to herself: "I'm going to follow that with my children. . . . She had that power." The lectures also captivated many of the high school students who raced to hear them after school. "I went to everything," one recalled. "Every chance I had I would go to hear her." Another who went said, "I sat on the edge of my chair; I just couldn't bear for the lectures to come to an end." All of these experiences had lasting effects. The persons cited here, and many others as well, reared their children in the "organic" way—absence of pressure or inappropriate demands and expectations, plenty of "child-centered" nurturing—and sent them to the school when the time came. Several became teachers themselves.[62]

In 1920 there were 853 persons in Fairhope; by 1930, 1,549 lived in the town. They were bound together by a strong sense of community that had emerged from the unique commitment to the single tax and to organic education. The two fused into a single unity to form the basis for a style of life that Fairhopers believed nurtured personal growth, unselfconsciousness, integration of aesthetic, artistic, and physical experiences in the daily routine, promoted participation in community affairs, and a sensitivity to community needs. With no rich and few who were poor, opposed to hierarchy and preten-

sion, given to easy and informal social intercourse, the
Fairhopers seemed to have internalized Marietta Johnson's mission as their own. There were many who lived
in the town who believed in neither the single tax nor
the Organic School—and the blacks were a segregated
community of their own—but the dominant tone was set
by the Fairhopers who believed in both and ordered
their lives accordingly. This augured well for the future
of the school and Marietta Johnson's mission.

In the long run, however, Mrs. Johnson knew that her
mission was not to be realized in Fairhope. Fairhope was
home, where she felt most comfortable, and her school
there was a palpable embodiment of her ideal. Moreover, she had made major accomplishments in securing
the kind of friendly community environment she
wanted for her ideas to flourish. But Fairhope was a
demonstration school. From the very beginning her
idea had been to use it as an example, an arguing point,
for converting the rest of the nation. Now, in the 1920s
when a new surge of progressive educational interest
swept across the country, she would have her last effort
at converting her mission into success.

"Mrs. Johnson left for the West Monday," the *Courier*
reported in the autumn of 1921. "Her lecture engagements will keep her so busy that it may be the New Year
before she returns to us." Such reports were common-
place throughout the twenties so that Fairhopers developed much pride in their fellow colonist who spread
Fairhope's fame wherever she went. For her, too, there
must have been satisfactions. She had a powerful effect
on her audiences, converting the skeptical and energizing the faithful. Her scrapbook is full of clippings testi-
fying to the praise she won. A New York reporter wrote
that Dewey ranked her at the top of the list of American
progressive educators, a California professor trum-

peted her coming to Berkeley as "a great public event," and a popular magazine writer described her as "perhaps the most courageous of all our educational nonconformers." On four occasions she was a featured speaker at international conferences—Cambridge, England, 1922; Heidelberg, Germany, 1925; Locarno, Switzerland, 1927; and Dublin, Ireland, 1933. Meanwhile, she encouraged and oversaw the establishment of still more satellite schools. By the early thirties she had been midwife to at least nine organic schools, acting as director of some, staffing most with teachers she had trained, and regularly visiting almost all. One journal identified her as "the founder of the famous Fairhope schools," thus giving strength to the image of her as a national educational leader and to Fairhope as the home of a national movement.[63]

At the end of the twenties Agnes de Lima, herself a prominent authority on progressive education, described Marietta Johnson as a "seasoned rebel" with a "gift for oratory and a rich and overflowing personality" who had carried the message of organic education "by word of mouth from one end of the country to another." Now, de Lima wrote, she was seeking a wider audience with the publication of her first book, *Youth in a World of Men*. Many of the reviews were flattering and a favorable reception was encouraged by the endorsements of the artist Rockwell Kent, who designed the cover, and the Columbia historian James Harvey Robinson, who greeted it with "enthusiasm and hearty approval." Nonetheless, the book was a disappointment to many of Mrs. Johnson's friends and it failed to make a significant mark in the literature of progressive education. Grace Rotzel—than whom there was no more devoted disciple—confessed her disappointment. Marietta Johnson simply "wasn't an intellectual," she sighed. De Lima had been

equally forthright in her review, describing the book as
"quite naive and entirely innocent of expert or studied
thinking."[64]

Both of these friendly critics were correct: Mrs.
Johnson was not an intellectual. Her central passion
was not the life of the mind, and her book lacked historical perspective, scholarly context, and even the texture of experience. This last defect was surprising, yet
one finds almost nothing about the Organic School and
its pupils. It was precisely the lack of such texture that
de Lima regretted for she believed that had Mrs. Johnson written about the lives of her students she would
have made a powerful case for her theories. Instead,
*Youth in a World of Men* was an unsuccessful attempt to
convert Mrs. Johnson's popular lectures into printed
narrative and exhortation. A visitor to the winter
course once wrote that Mrs. Johnson "at once charms
and kindles" and went on to say that "you can't express
in words what she is, nor yet what she does to you. But
to start with she makes me feel as though my mind had
been swept and as though I could begin to put my
house in order from the ground up." For most people
that effect was missing in the book. Instead, one
found—in bald statement and utter simplicity of argument—the case for organic education as the answer to
virtually every personal and social problem. Arrested
development accounted for greed, crime, economic in-
equality, and war. The book offered a blueprint, vague
in some of its outlines, for the rearing and educating of
children so that they would become truly socialized individuals, their powers developed, their cooperative
spirits nurtured, and their commitment to their fellow
human beings established. Reading the book with the
sympathy of a disciple, Grace Rotzel explained, one
could hear Marietta's voice clearly so that one would be

taken over the naïve spots. Without that sympathy, one
was unlikely to be moved or persuaded.[65]

Throughout the 1920s Mrs. Johnson's missionary
work—her lecturing, the Greenwich summer school,
the creation of satellite schools, and her writing—was
coordinated, encouraged, and modestly financed by the
Fairhope Educational Foundation. At the end of the
decade there were 215 members of the foundation, almost half of whom were from Greenwich and New York
City. Most of the foundation members, having long
since given up the idea of transplanting Mrs. Johnson to
the North, also vigorously supported the Fairhope
school. The foundation existed, as one bulletin accu-
rately put it, "To Sustain and Extend the Educational
Work of Marietta L. Johnson." May Lanier was regularly elected president and her friendship with Mrs.
Johnson deepened every year. *Youth in a World of Men*
was dedicated to her. Fund-raising campaigns for the
Fairhope school were constant topics of conversation at
foundation meetings, but no formula for success was
ever discovered. In 1930 Mrs. Lanier began a campaign
for a $250,000 endowment "for Mrs. Johnson's labora-
tory and . . . the Fairhope Idea," but the responses were
disappointing. That same year a board member wrote
confidentially that "the whole future of the Fairhope
foundation seems to me very doubtful but it is such a
part of Mrs. Johnson's life that I am in favor of keeping
it going as strong as possible and hope some of her plans
will work out." For the next few years the correspondence over money matters reveals no improvement.
Mrs. Johnson wrote to the secretary of the foundation
in the summer of 1931 about the poor enrollment at
Greenwich and of "the financial outlook [which] is so
very poor." May Lanier complained affectionately that
"the dear lady hates the inconvenience of business

procedure," and it is true that Mrs. Johnson preferred the grand gesture to the prosaic financial report. As the depression deepened, she wrote Alfred Stern at the Rosenwald Foundation. Peace and constructive social change, not war and revolution, were crucial to the nation; organic education offered the way to both, she said, urging Sloan to commit Rosenwald funds to the Fairhope school.[66]

In 1932 the Organic School celebrated its twenty-fifth anniversary. The *New York Times,* a friendly chronicler for two decades, took note of the event. For many years now the school had been "a mecca for teachers eager to learn of its methods" and it had also set a pattern "for about a dozen other schools in various parts of the country." After twenty-five years it had graduated enough students so that some measure of its success was possible. Organic graduates had done well, the *Times* reported, and educators such as President Arthur Morgan of Antioch and President Hamilton Holt of Rollins prized them for their zest and the "freshness of their intellectual attack." Mrs. Johnson was pleased, but not surprised, by these results; however, she took special pride in the fact that no students or teachers had ever had a nervous breakdown—this, she said, was more significant than the good records they had made at such places as Yale and MIT.[67]

Approving and intended to be helpful, the *Times* article passed silently over the financial crisis that had paralyzed the Fairhope Educational Foundation and was threatening to cripple the school as well. It mentioned the founding of satellite schools, but did not note that none had been started in recent years. A prescient observer would have seen the receding of the Fairhope influence and a turning inward by its diminishing number of friends to save the mother school in its moment of greatest crisis. Just two months after the *Times* article appeared, Mrs. Johnson published an "urgent appeal" in the *Courier.* "After a substantial reduction in the teachers' salaries, we still find ourselves with a very embarrassing deficit at the close of the session," she wrote. She called upon every friend of the school to contribute twenty-five dollars so that the school might pay its debts and continue another year.[68]

The school opened again in September, just as it had every fall for the previous quarter-century, but Mrs. Johnson's concerns had not been removed. "We have been fools enough to open the school again even in the face of the most forbidding conditions," she wrote privately. "We are reducing our home department almost to a 'cooperative commonwealth,' [and] everybody is helping with dishes and sweeping, and so forth. . . . We are trying to conduct the school with as little outlay of money as possible since, as you know, we are getting in very, very little."[69]

The school had been faced with crisis before, and on more than one occasion there had been doubts about whether it would open. The national depression, however, brought about a fundamental structural change. During the halcyon years of the twenties virtually all of the school's revenue came from outside Fairhope— from Mrs. Johnson's lecture tours, from the Fairhope Educational Foundation, and from the boarding students. All of these sources of income were now drying up. The decline in the number of boarding students was especially ominous. The net profit on the boarding department had ranged from $9,000 to $17,000 between 1925 and 1930; in 1933–34 it was $3,923, and it went down steadily to a low of $1,171 in 1937–38. "Catastrophe befell the school," one of its teachers later wrote, citing in particular the "depletion of the population of the boarding department." Salaries plummeted and in 1933 the *New York Times,* still following the school's history with sympathy, wrote that "the teachers have offered to work with greatly reduced salaries, with the understanding that if the school is unable to pay them it will be under no financial obligation to them for the rest of the year."[70]

Mrs. Johnson's correspondence chronicles the uneven struggle to survive. "Last spring you saved our lives," she wrote to a patron in 1935. "There certainly would not be an Organic School in Fairhope this year if it had not been for your timely aid." Two letters the next year reflect deepening gloom: "The depression is not over with us. . . . We have had only eleven boarders this winter, and many of them for only part time. . . . The plant is terribly run down and much money is needed for restoration." And: "My own income had been so terribly decreased by reduced interest that I am at a loss quite often to know which way to turn for my regular expenses." In 1937 she told a supporter who urged her to advertise the school that "any advertising that is done must be done personally and I am unable to manage it." To her son, Clifford Ernest, she wrote that "every penny we can get . . . will come in mighty handy at this time." And to an old Greenwich patron she wrote plaintively, "We are now in the last ditch. Something surely must happen or it will be our last year."[71]

Somehow she managed to keep the doors open. She dipped into her own savings from time to time—those close to her say she was the "anonymous donor" who saved the school more than once—and by 1936 she was writing hopefully about a new fund-raising campaign, firing off letters to her wealthy and influential friends, and turning more insistently to Fairhope residents for small contributions. Optimism crept into her letters when she could see her way clear to carrying on: "I came home with so much joy and hope and confidence that now I am ready to announce that the school will go on," she wrote in the spring of 1937, and early in 1938 she told a Greenwich friend that she had expected to close down after the thirtieth year, "but the Parent Teachers Round Table decided to try to raise one hundred contributions of fifty dollars each. . . . This turned the tide and now we are all pepped up to preserve this work."[72]

She traveled less in the last years, and at the urging of friends she wrote another book which they hoped would be a history of the school. She called it "Thirty Years with an Idea," but it was discursive, repetitive, and, like her first book, told little about the school itself. No publisher would take it on. "It seems to offer nothing new in progressive education," one editor commented. Mrs. Johnson seemed resigned. "It really doesn't matter if it is ever published," she wrote to her friend who was shepherding the manuscript around New York.[73]

Since 1930 she had been visibly aging, or so her closest associates thought. Many of them ascribed the change to the death of Charles Rabold, her assistant director and the person on whom she depended to take over from her. His death seemed to undermine the "freshness of attack that she had had," one person observed. Another noted that Rabold's death "killed her spirits," that she "slipped very much" after he died. With Rabold gone, her manuscript rejected, the Fairhope Educational Foundation defunct, and her old friends unable to help her out as they had in the past, she must have found herself increasingly isolated. Her old Progressive Education Association colleague Stanwood Cobb, once a disciple, had changed his mind about her. She was "on the radical edge, the fanatic fringe," he confided in a later interview. She had "lapsed into one of the also-rans."[74]

As worries mounted and friends fell away, her health worsened. She suffered from angina for several years before she had the first heart attack in the summer of 1937. She recovered slowly and some of her disciples and close friends found her to be despondent, troubled by the bleakness of the school's future. "I didn't see the gleam in her eyes," one man who was close to her recalls, "I didn't see her look in the fireplace as she had in the past." As if poor health were not enough, she cried out on occasion that she feared she was losing her mind—a terror that she knew had seized her old comrades E. B. Gaston and Marie Howland before her. Friends watched with apprehension as she turned to spiritual answers, especially the "I Am" movement. She wrote to Fanny Hoggson that she was "practicing the raising of my consciousness" and to May Lanier that she spent "a great deal of time reading Troward and other things pertaining to man's relation to the Universe." She found it all "a great comfort to me and I believe it is helping."[75]

Her fatal heart attack came in 1938, two days before Christmas. She was seventy-four. The funeral was held the following Monday, the day after Christmas, in Comings Hall, the large school auditorium and community gathering place that had been her church and her pulpit. There was a heavy downpour in the morning, but the hall was overflowing with townspeople come to mourn, find comfort in each other's company, and sing for one last time in her presence the song "Fairhope" that she had led them in singing at the close of so many meetings.[76]

The townspeople who filled Comings Hall for her funeral would have been shocked to hear Marietta Johnson called an also-ran, but the old-timers would have had no problem including her among those on the "radical edge," even if that were to be called the "fanatic fringe." The radical edge, after all, was where she had wanted to be for thirty years and that was where a good Fairhoper felt most comfortable. Where else should one be?

The students who had attended Marietta Johnson's Organic School would have found it especially difficult to look on their idol as an also-ran. Their testimony—in letters, interviews, casual conversation, and published recollections—is strikingly similar: they liked school, looked upon it as the most positive force in their lives, and they more often than not ended up as missionaries of organic education themselves. Margaret Mead, who confessed that her sister Priscilla had not taken to organic education ("You aren't meant to like school," she said), had a different story for sister Elizabeth. "At Fairhope," she wrote, Elizabeth "learned practically nothing at all—except how to teach, how to waken children to enthusiasm, and how to treat each individual as a person. This she has carried all through her life." Harold Riegger, a member of the class of 1931, felt so passionately about Mrs. Johnson's influence on him that he required his publisher to include *Youth in a World of Men* in the bibliography of his third book as a way of acknowledging his indebtedness. A noted potter and author, Riegger believes the school "had a profound influence on my thinking, development and life and I am forever thankful that I went there." A woman who graduated from the school, took the teachers' training course, and taught for a while in the Hood River, Oregon, satellite school, had caught all of Mrs. Johnson's enthusiasm: "She made you feel that you were part of something big and wonderful, that teaching was the most important job in the world, and . . . you could change the whole universe with what you did with these children."[77] Lifelong influences like these belie Cobb's facile also-ran label.

Cobb was right that she was an also-ran in the sense that she had not restructured American education and, in fact, was no longer a prominent force in it. She had recently been made an honorary lifetime vice-president of the Progressive Education Association, and when Fairhopers arranged a testimonial evening for her a month before she died, the outpouring of praise might have led one to look on her as a major influence. Novelist Dorothy Canfield Fisher said that her work was "of golden and lasting value," and as the master of ceremonies read from "a great sheaf" of papers conveying praise, the Fairhopers must have glowed with satisfaction. Still, Cobb had a point: the progressive education movement had long since steered wide of Marietta Johnson's vision of a new social order and the modest national movement she had once headed was now in disarray, the victim of economic depression, old age, and shifting national priorities.[78]

What had not changed was the profound difference she had made in the lives of so many people—her students, fellow teachers, friends, and disciples. They would be the lasting legacy of her mission, reminders of a forgotten history and a woman with much hope for her fellows.

And what of her? Remarkably, she maintained to the end the freshness, the simplicity, and the confidence that had set her apart all of her life. In the face of vanishing support, declining health, and deepening anxieties, she somehow managed to burst out of her encirclement with volleys of optimism and reaffirmation. She remonstrated with national single-taxers and leaders of the Progressive Education Association to work for common goals; she cheered up former students and told them she was counting on them to take over the school when she was gone; and she reiterated the old verities. "You must remember," she wrote in one of her letters, "that credits, recognitions, honorable mentions, etc., are the most difficult things in the world to overcome," ruing the fact that many progressive schools were offenders in this regard. "I do hope you . . . are studying Henry George," she concluded. "Do . . . use your influence for fundamental justice in economics."[79]

A woman who heard Marietta Johnson give her last speech—breathless with exhaustion—to a group of "third life" mothers remembers the occasion with awe. "She made it through. . . . What a forceful person she was! She didn't give up! She kept on to the very end. It was wonderful, wasn't it? . . . And still giving out her principles! Wasn't it wonderful?"[80]

# Notes

## ONE
### The Discovery of Nancy Lewis

1. Minutes, Fairhope Industrial Association (FIA), January 22, February 2, 7, 1895.

2. Minutes, FIA, February 7, 23, March 9, 1895; Agreement Between Fairhope Industrial Association and Nancy Lewis, February 12, 1895.

3. Paul M. Gaston, "Gaston, Ernest B.," in Alden Whitman (ed.), *Great American Reformers* (New York, 1984), pp. 342–43.

4. E. B. Gaston, "True Co-operative Individualism: An Argument on the Plan of Fairhope Industrial Association," *Liberty Bell,* April 28, 1894.

5. The colonies that most interested him were Kaweah, in Tulare County, California, and the Credit Foncier of Sinaloa, in Topolobampo, Sinaloa Province, Mexico. His own projected colony was to be called the National Cooperative Company and was intended to be in Louisiana.

6. Henry George, *Progress and Poverty* (New York, 1960; 1879), p. 328.

7. Interview, C. A. Gaston, October 12, 1978.

8. E. B. Gaston to H. Olerich, November 4, 1890, Fairhope Single Tax Colony Archives (hereinafter cited as FSTC Archives).

9. *Fairhope Courier,* April 1, 1898.

10. Ibid., August 21, 1908.

11. Ibid., February 15, 1903.

12. Ibid., September 1, 1903.

13. Ibid., February 1, 1899.

14. Ibid., August 25, 1911; see also May 15, 1904, and January 19, 1923.

15. Ibid., June 12, 1925.

16. The biographical data are based on a close reading of the Baldwin County, Battles Precinct, manuscript censuses of 1870, 1880, and 1900. The 1850 and 1860 Lauderdale County, Mississippi, manuscript censuses offer tantalizing possibilities: one white man named Lewis owned nineteen slaves, two of whom were the ages and color of Nancy and John. The case of the Virginia master who sold slaves South to escape his own financial slavery is described in Kenneth M. Stampp, *The Peculiar Institution* (New York, 1956), pp. 269–71.

17. Quoted in Leon F. Litwack, *Been in the Storm So Long: The Aftermath of Slavery* (New York, 1979), p. 401.

18. Quoted in ibid.

19. E. B. Gaston to H. Olerich, November 4, 1890, FSTC Archives; George, *Progress and Poverty,* p. 334.

20. Vernon Lane Wharton, *The Negro in Mississippi, 1865–1890* (Chapel Hill, 1947), p. 59.

21. Baldwin County Deed Book M, pp. 544–46, 549–50.

22. My search at the courthouse turned up tax records for 1882, 1889, 1890, 1891, 1892, 1894, and 1895. The "annual levies" figures cited in the text are derived from these records.

23. Interview, Rosetta Lewis, October 21, 1980.

24. Charles Hill, "Address . . . ," in *Twenty-Sixth Anniversary, Fairhope Single Tax Colony: Addresses, Messages, History, Songs* (Fairhope, 1921), pp. 9–10.

25. Baldwin County Tax Book, 1895; Interview, Rosetta Lewis; *Fairhope Courier,* June 1, 1904.

26. Minutes, FIA, June 10, 1895.

27. Interview, Rosetta Lewis; Sales of Real Estate for Unpaid Taxes, Baldwin County, I, p. 94; Deed Book X, pp. 37–39, 43–45.

28. *Fairhope Courier,* July 22, 1910.

# TWO
## The Odyssey of Marie Howland

1. *Fairhope Courier,* September 23, 1921.

2. Ibid., May 15, 1904.

3. Marie Howland to Edmund Clarence Stedman, September 27, 1907, Stedman Papers, Columbia University Library.

4. Ray P. Reynolds, *Cat's Paw Utopia* (El Cajon, Calif., 1972); Rob-

ert S. Fogarty, "The Familistère: Radical Reform Through Cooperative Enterprise," in Marie Howland, *The Familistère: A Novel,* 3rd ed.
(Philadelphia, 1975); Lynda Morgan, " 'A Feast of Reason and a
Flow of Soul': Marie Howland, Career Reformer, 1836–1921" (unpublished seminar paper, University of Virginia, 1980); Dolores
Hayden, *The Grand Domestic Revolution: A History of Feminist Designs
for American Homes, Neighborhoods, and Cities* (Cambridge, Mass.,
1981). Hayden's book and the favorable response to it are likely to
encourage students to give Howland the attention she deserves. See,
for example, Nancy F. Cott, "The House of Feminism," *New York
Review of Books,* March 17, 1983, pp. 36–40.

   5. Interview, Ronald Mershon, July 13, 1981; Interview, Helenbelle Lucier Rockwell, August 3, 1979.

   6. Calvin Trillin, "U.S. Journal: Fairhope, Ala.," *New Yorker,* June
11, 1979, p. 80.

   7. *Fairhope Courier,* May 1, 1899.

   8. According to the 1840 manuscript census, there were 1,754 persons in Lebanon; 1,037 of them were employed, 80.4 percent in agri-
culture. The comment on her happy childhood comes from an 1886
letter in the files of Ray P. Reynolds; the others are from a letter she
wrote to E. H. Cheney that appeared in the *Granite State Free Press*
(Lebanon), June 19, 1874, a source of considerable information about
her early years in Lebanon. See also Carrie E. Willie to Library of
Congress, August 10, 1951, Marie Howland Collection, Library of
Congress, and Edward Howland, "Marie Howland, The Translator
of Godin's Social Solutions," *Social Solutions* 2 (May 28, 1886): 1–4.
The manuscript census of 1850 is the only source for locating Marie in
Manchester in 1850 and her sisters in nearby Barnstead.

   9. Benita Eisler, ed., *The Lowell Offering: Writings by New England
Mill Women (1840–1845)* (New York, 1977), pp. 15–26.

   10. *Granite State Free Press,* June 19, 1874; Thomas Dublin, *Women
at Work: The Transformation of Work and Community in Lowell, Massachusetts, 1826–1860* (New York, 1979), pp. 139–41; Edward
Howland, "Marie Howland," p. 2.

   11. *Granite State Free Press,* May 29, 1874.

   12. Charles Dickens, *American Notes and Pictures from Italy* (London,
1957; 1842), pp. 88–90; Carroll S. Rosenberg, "Protestants and Five
Pointers: The Five Points House of Industry, 1850–1870," *New York
Historical Society Quarterly* 48 (October, 1964): 327; Herbert Asbury,
*The Gangs of New York: An Informal History of the Underworld* (New York,

1928), p. 10; Ladies of the Mission, *The Old Brewery, and the New Mission House at Five Points* (New York, 1854), p. 152; *Fairhope Courier*, August 15, 1902. See also Edward K. Spann, *The New Metropolis: New York City, 1840–1857* (New York, 1981), pp. 274–75; and Carroll S. Rosenberg, *Religion and the Rise of the American City: The New York City Mission Movement, 1812–1870* (Ithaca, 1971), chap. 8.

13. Marie Howland, "Biographical Sketch of Edward Howland" (typescript, 1891, originally published in the *Credit Foncier of Sinaloa*), pp. 48–50, Fairhope Public Library; Vernon Loggins, *Where the Word Ends: The Life of Louis Moreau Gottschalk* (Baton Rouge, 1958), pp. 151–79; *New York Daily Tribune*, August 15, November 17, 27, 1855; *New York Atlas*, November 11, 1855; George C. D. Odell, *Annals of the New York Stage*, 16 vols. (New York, 1927–49), 6: 418, 493.

14. Loggins, *Life of Gottschalk*, pp. 168–69; Alastor [Ada Clare], "The Pangs of Despised Love," *New York Atlas*, December 28, 1856.

15. Marie Howland, "Biographical Sketch of Edward Howland," pp. 49–50.

16. Marie Howland to Edmund Clarence Stedman, April 21, 1907.

17. Madeleine B. Stern, *The Pantarch: A Biography of Stephen Pearl Andrews* (Austin, Texas, 1968), pp. 87–91; James J. Martin, *Men Against the State: The Expositors of Individualist Anarchism in America, 1827–1908* (DeKalb, Ill., 1953), pp. 165–66.

18. *New York Daily Tribune*, October 16, 1855.

19. Ibid. The Club was discussed in news reports, editorials, and letters to the editor of the *Tribune*. See issues of October 16, 19, and 24. The place was raided on October 18 and Brisbane was among those arrested. Charges were dropped the next day. A long description from the *New York Times*, October 10, 1855, is reprinted, along with commentary, in Taylor Stoehr (ed.), *Free Love in America: A Documentary History* (New York, 1979), pp. 319–31.

20. Hal Sears, *The Sex Radicals: Free Love in High Victorian America* (Lawrence, Kans., 1977), p. 22.

21. Hayden, *Grand Domestic Revolution*, p. 94.

22. Marie Howland to Edmund Clarence Stedman, April 21, 1907.

23. Marie Howland to Edmund Clarence Stedman, September 27, 1907.

24. Brook Farm and the North American Phalanx were the two experiments best known to Marie Howland. She visited the latter once. On Fourier's thought, see Nicholas V. Riasonovsky, *The Teach-*

*ing of Charles Fourier* (Berkeley, 1969); Frank E. Manuel and Fritzie P. Manuel, *Utopian Thought in the Western World* (Cambridge, Mass., 1979), esp. chap. 27; David Zeldin, *The Educational Ideas of Charles Fourier (1772–1837)* (London, 1969); and Donald Drew Egbert, *Social Radicalism and the Arts, Western Europe: A Cultural History from the French Revolution to 1968* (New York, 1970), esp. chap. 3. Marie very likely read the work on Fourier by his chief American disciple and her friend Albert Brisbane. See Brisbane, *Association; or, A Concise Exposition of the Practical Part of Fourier's Social Science* (New York, 1843).

25. Riasonovsky, *The Teaching of Charles Fourier*, p. 52.

26. Laura Stedman and George M. Gould, *Life and Letters of Edmund Clarence Stedman*, 2 vols. (New York, 1910), 1: 154–57.

27. *New York Times*, June 22, 1858.

28. Ibid., September 21, 1860.

29. Stedman and Gould, *Life and Letters of Stedman*, 1: 160.

30. Marie Howland to Edmund Clarence Stedman, April 21, 1907.

31. Riasonovsky, *The Teaching of Charles Fourier*, p. 52.

32. Marie wrote to Stedman some years later, probably in 1889, from Topolobampo: "My conscience has always troubled me about him (this is confidential) for he was so magnanimous. I like to think of all his goodness and even wear the dresses he liked best." Marie Howland to Edmund Clarence Stedman, n.d. Case died in the spring of 1892 and left Marie a $5,000 legacy which was a vital source of support for the rest of her life. She wrote to Stedman about it: "It is not often that the affection of a friend—rare indeed a husband's—survives such rude tests. But in truth, Lion & I were better friends when we had obtained the divorce! We corresponded to within ten days of his death." Marie Howland to Edmund Clarence Stedman, December 16, 1893. See also Marie Howland to Anna Hoffman, December 6, 1915, C. B. Hoffman Collection, University of Kansas.

33. Mary Heath Lee, "Edward Howland—A Biographical Sketch" (manuscript, 1923?), Fairhope Public Library; Edmund Clarence Stedman, *An American Anthology, 1787–1899* (Boston, 1900), p. 802; Marie Howland, "Biographical Sketch of Edward Howland." Edward was born September 15, 1832.

34. Marie Howland, "Biographical Sketch of Edward Howland," pp. 16, 20.

35. Marie Howland to Edmund Clarence Stedman, June 21,

1894. Marie's niece Mabel, the daughter of her sister Ada, later married Aubrey, the son of Ada Clare and Gottschalk.

36. Marie Howland to Edmund Clarence Stedman, April 21, 1907.

37. Ibid.; Certificate, Board of Education of the City of New York Normal Schools, July 14, 1859, Howland Collection, Fairhope Single Tax Corporation Archives; Thomas Boese, *Public Education in the City of New York: Its History, Condition, and Statistics* (New York, 1869), pp. 144–45.

38. Edward Howland, "Marie Howland," p. 2; *Fairhope Courier,* August 31, 1906; *Granite State Free Press,* June 19, 1874.

39. Morgan, "Marie Howland," p. 4.

40. William Winter, *Old Friends: Being Literary Recollections of Other Days* (New York, 1909), p. 57.

41. Stedman and Gould, *Life and Letters of Stedman,* 1: 208; Marie Howland, "Biographical Sketch of Edward Howland," p. 3.

42. *New York Saturday Press,* January 29, 1859.

43. For descriptions of Pfaff's Cellar and the social life there, see Winter, *Old Friends,* pp. 64, 82; Stedman and Gould, *Life and Letters of Stedman,* 1: 208–209; Francis Wolle, *Fitz-James O'Brien, A Literary Bohemian of the Eighteen-Fifties* (Boulder, 1944), pp. 92–93, 124; Allen Lesser, *Enchanting Rebel: The Secret of Adah Isaacs Menken* (New York, 1947), p. 66; Loggins, *Life of Gottschalk,* pp. 186–87; and Albert Parry, *Garrets and Pretenders: A History of Bohemianism in America* (New York, 1960; 1933), pp. 14–61.

44. Marie Howland to Edmund Clarence Stedman, April 21, 1907; Marie Howland, "Biographical Sketch of Edward Howland," p. 3.

45. *Fairhope Courier,* May 1, 1900, March 1, 1907; Edward Howland, "Marie Howland," pp. 2–3; Lee, "Edward Howland," p. 1; Marie Howland, "Biographical Sketch of Edward Howland," pp. 7–9, 43–47, 72.

46. Marie Howland, "Biographical sketch of Edward Howland," pp. 6–11.

47. Jean-Baptiste André Godin, *Social Solutions,* trans. Marie Howland (New York, 1886), pp. 219–20, 224–25. The book was published in French in 1871.

48. Edward Howland, "The Social Palace at Guise," *Harper's New Monthly Magazine* 44 (April 1872): 701–16; Marie Howland, "The Festival of Labor [at Guise]," *Overland Monthly* 1 (March 1883): 304–308.

49. Marie Howland, "Biographical Sketch of Edward Howland,"

pp. 30–31; Edward Howland, *Grant as a Soldier and Statesman: Being a Succinct History of his Military and Civil Career* (Hartford, Conn., 1868).

50. Marie Howland, "Torricelli," *Harper's New Monthly Magazine* 66 (March 1883): 600, 602; Marie Howland, "Biographical Sketch of Edward Howland," p. 73; Marie Howland to Edmund Clarence Stedman, December 4, 1895; *Fairhope Courier*, November 9, 1906.

51. "Modern Bee Culture," *Harper's New Monthly Magazine* 61 (October 1880): 777–80; "Musical Notation," *Lippincott's Monthly Magazine* 22 (August 1878): 232–41; "Education in Japan," *The Californian* 2 (October 1880): 348–53; "The Patrons of Husbandry," *Lippincott's Monthly Magazine* 12 (September 1873): 338–42; "A Lady's Enterprise," *Harper's New Monthly Magazine* 47 (October 1873): 641–51; "Lieber and Niebuhr," *Harper's New Monthly Magazine* 48 (December 1883): 63–65; and "The Poor Capitalists," *Galaxy* 3 (January 1867): 197–201.

52. *Harper's New Monthly Magazine* 49 (August 1874): 443.

53. Marie Howland, *The Familistère: A Novel* (Philadelphia, 1975; 1874), pp. 358–59. Entitled *Papa's Own Girl* in the first (1874) and second (1885) editions, it was called *The Familistère* in the third (1918) edition.

54. Ibid., pp. 67, 96; Morgan, "Marie Howland," p. 10; *Granite State Free Press,* June 5, 1874.

55. Ada Clare's son Aubrey lived with Marie often while his mother was on tour as an actress with her husband, Frank Noyes. Ada Clare died of hydrophobia in 1874 and was buried at Casa Tonti in a grave beside her infant daughter Agnes. An imaginative historian or a novelist with an appetite for patient research would find much pleasure in writing a book about the relationship of Marie and Ada Clare. *New York Daily Tribune*, March 3, 1874; Marie Howland to Edmund Clarence Stedman, April 21, 1907; *Fairhope Courier*, November 9, 1906; Parry, *Garrets and Pretenders*, pp. 359–60.

56. Marie Howland to Edmund Clarence Stedman, December 25, 1896. See also Marie Howland, "Biographical Sketch of Edward Howland," pp. 15–16.

57. Quoted in Hayden, *Grand Domestic Revolution*, p. 105.

58. The motto, written by Owen, was on the masthead of the colony organ, *Credit Foncier of Sinaloa;* Hayden, *Grand Domestic Revolution*, p. 106.

59. Albert Owen, *Integral Co-Operation: Its Practical Operation* (New York, 1885).

60. Marie Howland to Edmund Clarence Stedman, April 21, 1907. *Social Solutions* had been translated over a dozen years before Marie could find a publisher for it. John Lovell brought it out in 1886. See Madeleine B. Stern, *Imprints in History: Book Publishers and American Frontiers* (Bloomington, Ind., 1956), pp. 268–69. Marie wrote frequently in the *Courier* about how much this book meant to her and to Edward. Shortly before they left Casa Tonti, Godin died. Marie wote of him that he was "instituting a new destiny for the laboring millions of the earth by giving them the right to retain a fair share of the result of their labor." *Credit Foncier of Sinaloa,* February 7, 1888.

61. Marie Howland to Edmund Clarence Stedman, November 1887, August 24, 1888, June 14, 1890.

62. *Credit Foncier of Sinaloa,* December 27, 1890.

63. Marie Howland to Edmund Clarence Stedman, June 18, 1890.

64. *Credit Foncier of Sinaloa,* March 15, 1890, July 15, 1891.

65. Harriet E. Standfast, "To The Directors and Fellow Colonists of the Credit Foncier Co.," June 10, 1889, copy supplied by California State University, Fresno.

66. Henry Standfast, "To the Directors and Fellow Colonists of the Credit Foncier Company," June 10, 1889, copy supplied by California State University, Fresno.

67. Quoted in Reynolds, *Cat's Paw Utopia,* p. 87. Reynolds's sprightly history is the basic source for Marie's Mexican years.

68. Ibid., pp. 77–83. Reynolds states that letters from Mrs. Hoffman to Owen prove that Marie and Hoffman had an affair in Mexico. I have not read these letters.

69. *Fairhope Courier,* July 1, 1898.

70. Ibid., October 1, 1898, February 1, 1899.

71. J. Bellangee to E. B. Gaston, December 3, 1896, FSTC Archives; *Fairhope Courier,* January 15, 1899.

72. This portrait of Fairhope women is based on biographical data in the *Courier;* the manuscript census; E. B. Gaston's correspondence; Morgan, "Marie Howland"; and Ann-Marie Bolton, "Women of Fairhope, 1894–1903" (unpublished seminar paper, University of Virginia, 1982). A fuller description will appear in my forthcoming history of Fairhope.

73. *Fairhope Courier,* November 15, 1895.

74. Ibid., May 1, 1903, May 5, 1905, June 2, 1905, November 10, 1905.

75. Ibid., June 21, 1907.

76. *Credit Foncier of Sinaloa,* July 1, 1890.

77. Joseph Fels to E. B. Gaston, April 25, 1899, FSTC Archives; *Fairhope Courier,* December 12, 1899, February 15, 1900, May 1, 1900, August 1, 1900.

78. Morgan, "Marie Howland," p. 50.

79. *Fairhope Courier,* November 1, 1899.

80. Minutes, Fairhope Industrial Association, May 25, 1896.

81. *Fairhope Courier,* August 15, 1899, January 1, 1900; Egbert, *Social Radicalism and the Arts,* p. 411.

82. *Fairhope Courier,* April 25, 1913, March 11, 1910, September 23, 1910, December 18, 1908, October 23, 1908, March 1, 1902, June 15, 1903, November 8, 1912.

83. Interview, Helenbelle Lucier Rockwell.

84. *Fairhope Courier,* August 23, 1907.

85. Ibid., March 1, 1912. "I am always ashamed to say 'women's rights,' " she wrote. "I wish the term had never been used. Sufficiently damning to the voters of the country that ever since the signing of the declaration of independence, these voters have maintained that equal political right is a matter of sex! What a disgrace to human intelligence!" Ibid., November 10, 1911.

86. *Credit Foncier of Sinaloa,* November 15, 1887; *Fairhope Courier,* July 22, 1910, May 24, 1907, June 15, 1899, September 6, 1907.

87. Ibid., December 22, 1906, July 22, 1910, June 1, 1906, April 1, 1904.

88. J. Bellangee to E. B. Gaston, July 16, 1894. On the relationship between the environment and communitarian reform, see Dolores Hayden, *Seven Utopias: The Architecture of Communitarian Socialism, 1790–1975* (Cambridge, Mass., 1976) and Egbert, *Social Radicalism and the Arts.* I was also helped by Susan Ulrich, "Fairhope: Utopian Planning and Idealism" (unpublished seminar paper, University of Virginia, 1982).

89. *Fairhope Courier,* January 1, 1895.

90. Paul E. and Blanche R. Alyea, *Fairhope, 1894–1954: The Story of a Single Tax Colony* (University, Ala., 1956), pp. 70–85.

91. *Fairhope Courier,* April 21, 1905, November 1, 1902. Of the Cherub she wrote: "Why he is a fine big boy and just as sweet and 'cunning' as ever. He goes through the Pines every day, usually with Cornelius, his elder brother—a noble little fellow is Cornie." Ibid., September 15, 1902.

92. Minutes, Fairhope Single Tax Corporation, September 19, 1921.

# THREE
*The Mission of Marietta Johnson*

1. Biographical data for Marietta Johnson's early years are scarce and sketchy. See the following: *Who Was Who in America,* 1:640; *Fairhope Courier,* December 29, 1938, and Golden Anniversary Issue, December 12, 1957; *Greenwich Press,* January 5, 1939; Esther Pierce Frederick, untitled biographical sketch, n.d., School of Organic Education Archives (hereafter cited as SOE Archives). I am further indebted for biographical information to Dr. Pierce Everett Frederick of Fairhope, one of Mrs. Johnson's grandnephews.

2. *Fairhope Courier,* January 1, 1903, September 1, 1904; Interview, Hazele Williams Payne, February 2, 1979; Hazele Williams Payne, "Mrs. Johnson's First Years Here" (unpublished memoir, n.d.), private collection; Esther Pierce Frederick, biographical sketch, SOE Archives.

3. Interview, Hazele Williams Payne.

4. Nathan Oppenheim, *The Development of the Child* (New York, 1898); *New York Times,* March 16, 1913.

5. U.S. Department of the Interior, *Report of the Commissioner of Education for 1886–1887* (Washington, 1890), p. 427; Rocco Eugene Zappone, "Progressive Education Reconsidered: The Intellectual Milieu of Marietta Johnson" (Master's thesis, University of Virginia, 1982), pp. 2–6; *New York Times,* March 16, 1913; Marietta L. Johnson, *Thirty Years with an Idea* (University, Ala., 1974), pp. xi–xii, 8–10.

6. Oppenheim, *Development of the Child,* pp. 7–9, 63–65, 103, 112.

7. Two good general histories of the progressive education movement are Robert Beck, "American Progressive Education, 1875–1930" (Ph.D. thesis, Yale University, 1942), and Lawrence A. Cremin, *The Transformation of the School: Progressivism in American Education, 1876–1957* (New York, 1961).

8. *Fairhope Courier,* January 1, 15, 1903, April 1, 1903, May 1, 1903.

9. Ibid., June 15, 1903, July 15, 1903, August 1, 1903, August 15, 1903, October 15, 1903, November 15, 1903, December 15, 1903.

10. Ibid., September 15, 1903, January 15, 1904.

11. Ibid., September 1, 1903, November 15, 1903, January 1, 1904, April 15, 1904, September 1, 1904.

12. Ibid., February 17, 1905.

13. Lydia J. Newcomb Comings, "An Intimate History of the

Early Days of the School of Organic Education" (typescript, 1939), private collection; S. H. Comings, *Pagan vs. Christian Civilizations: National Life and Permanence Dependent on Reform in Education* (Chicago, n.d.); *Fairhope Courier*, March 23, 1906, May 4, 1906, June 1, 8, 15, 29, 1906; Interview, Eleanor Coutant Nichols, July 20, 1979.

14. *Fairhope Courier*, July 6, 1906; C. Hanford Henderson, *Education and the Larger Life* (Boston, 1902), p. 97.

15. *Fairhope Courier*, May 10, 1907.

16. Ibid., April 1, 1904; L. J. N. Comings, "An Intimate History."

17. *Fairhope Courier*, November 8, 22, 29, 1907, December 6, 13, 1907, January 3, 1908; Interview, Hazele Williams Payne; Interview, Ronald Mershon, July 13, 1981.

18. L. J. N. Comings, "An Intimate History"; *Fairhope Courier*, January 31, 1908, February 7, 1908, March 8, 1908.

19. *Fairhope Courier*, June 12, 1908, December 18, 1908, January 1, 8, 1909; Joseph Fels to Marietta Johnson, January 13, 1909, FSTC Archives.

20. *Fairhope Courier*, April 10, 1908, August 7, 1908, August 8, 1910.

21. See texts of her speeches and statements on organic education and the relationship between it and the single tax in *Fairhope Courier*, January 28, 1910, November 17, 1911, and March 29, 1912.

22. John and Evelyn Dewey, *Schools of Tomorrow* (New York, 1915), p. 165; see also John Dewey, *The School and Society* (Chicago, 1899), pp. 19–44.

23. *Fairhope Courier*, October 15, 22, 1909, February 11, 1910; Helen Christine Bennett, "Mrs. Marietta Johnson," *American Magazine* 76 (July 1913): 31.

24. *Fairhope Courier*, June 30, 1911, July 14, 1911, April 11, 1913; *New York Times*, March 16, 1913.

25. Johnson, *Thirty Years with an Idea*, pp. 37–39; *New York Times*, July 27, 1913.

26. *New York Times*, July 27, 1913.

27. Johnson, *Thirty Years with an Idea*, p. 46.

28. *New Republic*, August 21, 1915, p. 64; *Fairhope Courier*, December 13, 26, 1913; Interview, Eleanor Coutant Nichols; *Survey*, May 16, 1914, p. 199.

29. Dewey and Dewey, *Schools of Tomorrow*, pp. 39–40.

30. Ibid., pp. 17–18, 21–23, 29–31, 34.

31. Ibid., pp. 39, 29.

32. Ibid., pp. 315–16.

33. *Fairhope Courier,* December 4, 1914, Marietta Johnson Scrapbook, SOE Archives; Interview, Dorothy Beiser Cain and Kenneth Cain, July 29, 1979; Interview, Eleanor Coutant Nichols; Interview, Ronald Mershon.

34. Patricia Albjerg Graham, *Progressive Education: From Arcady to Academe—A History of the Progressive Education Association, 1919–1955* (New York, 1967), pp. 17–20.

35. *Fairhope Courier,* July 11, 18, 1919, September 5, 12, 1919; Interview, Hazele Williams Payne; Interview, Ronald Mershon; Interview, Helenbelle Lucier Rockwell, August 3, 1979.

36. Interview, Mary Lee Pond, May 18, 1982; Johnson, *Thirty Years with an Idea,* p. 40; *Fairhope Courier,* December 29, 1938.

37. Marietta Johnson, "The School and the Child," in *Progressive Education Association in Convention, April 9 and 10, 1920* (Washington, 1920), pp. 7–16.

38. Ibid., pp. 19, 15.

39. *Bulletin of the Fairhope School Community,* No. 1, April 1925, and Martha Gruening interview with Mrs. Johnson in the *Paris Herald,* n.d., both in the Marietta Johnson Scrapbook.

40. Ibid. See also Johnson, *Thirty Years with an Idea,* pp. 51–70, and Marietta Johnson to Priscilla Richards, February 6, 1932. All Johnson correspondence, unless otherwise indicated, is in the SOE Archives.

41. Interview, Eleanor Coutant Nichols.

42. Lillian Rifkin Blumenfeld, *Consider the Child: A Book for Parents and Teachers* (Wilkes-Barre, Pa., 1978), pp. 2–3; Marietta Johnson to Harriet Wolf, June 5, 1935.

43. Blumenfeld, *Consider the Child,* pp. 2–3.

44. Interview, Mary Lee Pond; Interview, Claude Arnold, July 16, 1981; Interview, Lillian Totten, Claire Totten Gray, and Joyce Totten Bishop, September 2, 1978.

45. Marietta Johnson to Bertie T. White, August 28, 1933.

46. Marietta Johnson to Mrs. R. V. Merry, September 26, 1931.

47. Marietta Johnson to C. M. Donnelly, May 25, 1936.

48. Marietta Johnson to Adele Rosin, n.d.

49. "To Redeem the High School," *New Republic,* July 8, 1925, pp. 168–69, is an interesting article on curriculum reform at Fairhope. See also Willard H. Edwards, "The Social Sciences in the High School," *Survey,* March 15, 1929, pp. 786–87.

50. Marietta Johnson Scrapbook; *Mobile Register* description reprinted in *Fairhope Courier,* February 2, 1928; Anne Howard Chapin,

"The Child at Fairhope" (Unidentified magazine excerpt, 1927?), private collection; Interview, Adele Swedelius, August 5, 1979.

51. Agnes de Lima, "For the New Schools," *Survey*, September 15, 1929, p. 614; Johnson, *Thirty Years with an Idea*, pp. 105, 119.

52. For a discussion of the child's social development and her philosophy of socialization, see Marietta Johnson, *Youth in a World of Men* (New York, 1929), pp. 244–73.

53. *OHS Senior Outlet 1924*, pp. 12–13.

54. Interview, Elizabeth Brandenburg Slaughter, July 24, 1979; Interview, Eleanor Coutant Nichols; Interview, Dorothea Vanston Hedgcock, October 10, 1978; Interview, Craig T. Sheldon, August 5, 1979; *Fairhope Courier*, January 20, 1927; Sam and Helen Dyson, "Recollections: Organic School Activities" (typescript, October 27, 1957), Fairhope Public Library.

55. *Fairhope Courier*, April 9, 1920, and *passim*. Enrollment figures appeared irregularly in the *Courier;* school records do not have complete enrollment data. Interview, Mary Lee Pond.

56. Interview, Dorothea Vanston Hedgcock; Interview, Dorothy Beiser Cain and Kenneth Cain.

57. Grace Rotzel, "Foreword," *Thirty Years with an Idea*, p. viii; Grace Rotzel, *The School in Rose Valley* (Baltimore, 1971), p. ix; Interview, Grace Rotzel, May 13, 1977; Grace Rotzel to author, May 27, 1977.

58. Blumenfeld, *Consider the Child*, pp. 1–3; Paul Avrich, *The Modern School Movement: Anarchism and Education in the United States* (Princeton, 1980), pp. 57, 278, 287–88; K. Porter Aichele, "Wharton Esherick: An American Artist-Craftsman," in *The Wharton Esherick Museum: Studio and Collection* (Paoli, Pa., 1977), p. 5; Interview, Judson C. Gray, August 4, 1979; Interview, Dorothea Vanston Hedgcock; Interview, Dorothy Beiser Cain and Kenneth Cain; *Fairhope Courier*, February 13, 1930. I am indebted to Rebecca Penrose for the research she did for me on Rabold at the Cecil Sharp House in London.

59. *Fairhope Courier*, February 6, 1930.

60. *Cinagro, 1932*, p. 20; *New York Times*, April 26, 1925; *Fairhope Courier*, March 10, 1922, January 16, 1930. For an excellent account of the winter course, see Anna B. Nolan, "A Visit to Fairhope," *New Haven Teachers' Journal* 15 (June 1922): 6–11.

61. Interview, Elizabeth Brandenburg Slaughter; *Fairhope Courier*, February 2, 1927, March 10, 1927.

62. Interview, Louise Porter Rockwell, May 22, 1982; Interview,

Marie Beiser Redditt, July 25, 1979; Interview, Elizabeth Brandenburg Slaughter.

63. *Fairhope Courier,* October 28, 1921, December 24, 1920, October 12, 1933, June 7, 1934; Marietta Johnson Scrapbook; *Greenwich Press,* January 5, 1939; Marietta Johnson, "Breaking Our Educational Moulds," *World Tomorrow* 6 (October 1923): 295–97; Membership List, Fairhope Education Foundation, August 20, 1930, SOE Archives; Interview, Eleanor Coutant Nichols; Interview, Marie Beiser Redditt; Interview, Elizabeth Brandenburg Slaughter. The principal Fairhope satellite schools were the Edgewood School, Greenwich; the Fairhope School of Montclair, New Jersey; West Orange, New Jersey, school; the Orchard School, Indianapolis, Indiana; the Fairhope Country School, Ridgefield, Connecticut; Manhasset Bay School, Port Washington, Long Island; the Marietta Johnson School, Phoenix, Arizona; and the Hood River School, Hood River, Oregon. There were other schools inspired by her—one sees in her scrapbook, for example, items like this one: "One of my daughters is a disciple of Mrs. Johnson's and has a school in Winnetka [Illinois]. . . . They call it organic education"—and Mrs. Johnson wrote from time to time about various public schools where particular teachers or classrooms were trying out her ideas.

64. Johnson, *Youth in a World of Men;* de Lima, "For the New Schools," p. 614; *New York Times,* June 2, 1929; *Fairhope Courier,* May 30, 1929; *World Tomorrow* 13 (January 1930): 41; *Elementary School Journal* 30 (November 1929): 232; Interview, Grace Rotzel.

65. De Lima, "For the New Schools," p. 614; *Fairhope Courier,* February 18, 1926; Interview, Grace Rotzel.

66. Membership List, Fairhope Educational Foundation, August 20, 1930; *School and Life* [a publication of the Fairhope Educational Foundation] 1 (December 1920): 6; Minutes of the Meeting of the Executive Committee and Friends of the Fairhope Educational Foundation, January 20, 1928, SOE Archives; Mrs. Charles D. Lanier, draft of form letter launching $250,000 endowment campaign; Edward Yeomans to Everett, August 14, 1930; Marietta Johnson to Susan H. Gilman, July 10, 1931; May Lanier to Susan H. Gilman, July 7, 1931; Marietta Johnson to Alfred K. Stern, February 9, 1932; Marietta Johnson to Lucius Littaur, February 23, 1932.

67. *New York Times,* March 27, 1932.

68. *Fairhope Courier,* May 26, 1932.

69. Marietta Johnson to Margaret Sperry, September 26, 1932.

70. Financial Records, School of Organic Education; Mrs. John

Campbell, "Continuing the Story of Organic's Ups and Downs and Evidences of the School's Vitality" (manuscript, 1957), Fairhope Public Library; *New York Times*, April 2, 1933.

71. Marietta Johnson to Thomas P. Craig, November 19, 1935; Marietta Johnson to Tess S. McCall, May 8, 1936; Marietta Johnson to Grace Pierce, May 18, 1936; Marietta Johnson to Regina McGarrigle, November 7, 1937; Marietta Johnson to C. E. Johnson, September 28, 1937; Marietta Johnson to Noble Bartlett, January 23, 1937.

72. Interview, Dorothy Beiser Cain and Kenneth Cain; Interview, Marie Beiser Redditt; Marietta Johnson to Mr. and Mrs. S. B. Siddall, January 6, 1936; Marietta Johnson to Mrs. Arthur Stockstrom, March 2, 1937; Marietta Johnson to Mrs. Hooker, January 10, 1938.

73. The manuscript was eventually published by the University of Alabama Press in 1974, for the School of Organic Education. Miss Walker to Ruth Aley, June 30, 1938; Marietta Johnson to Irma Lederer, November 29, 1937.

74. Interview, Elizabeth Brandenburg Slaughter; Interview, Hazele Williams Payne; Graham, *Progressive Education*, p. 19n.

75. Renie Carlson Interview, Kenneth Cain, Spring 1981; Interview, Marvin Nichols, July 17, 1979; Marietta Johnson to Fanny Hoggson, October 18, 1937; Marietta Johnson to Mrs. Charles D. Lanier, September 23, 1937; Marietta Johnson to Laura C. Williams, June 1, 1937; Marietta Johnson to Elizabeth H. Sauter, July 20, 1937.

76. *Fairhope Courier*, December 29, 1938.

77. Margaret Mead, *Blackberry Winter: My Earlier Years* (New York, 1972), p. 70. Harold Riegger to Claire T. Gray, May 13, 1981; Riegger to Georgia Lloyd, April 2, 1981; Riegger to Dear Friends [Organic School classmates], May 1, 1978, copies in author's possession; Interview, Marie Beiser Redditt.

78. *Fairhope Courier*, February 25, 1937, December 1, 1938.

79. Marietta Johnson to Bolton Hall, September 15, 1936; Marietta Johnson to Frederick L. Redefer, November 23, 1937; Marietta Johnson to Carson Ryan, n.d.; Marietta Johnson to Georgia Lloyd, July 23, 1937; Marietta Johnson to Ruth Sundberg, October 18, 1937; Marietta Johnson to Hazel Lott, April 1, 1935.

80. Interview, Louise Porter Rockwell.

# Index

Rifkin, Lillian. *See* Blumenfeld,
  Lillian Rifkin
Robinson, James Harvey, 107
Rosenwald Foundation, 110
Rotzel, Grace: impressions of
  Organic School, 101–2;
  founder of Rose Valley
  School, 102; on Marietta
  Johnson's first book, 107,
  108–9
Rousseau, Jean Jacques, 71, 86
Ruskin colony, 58

St. Cloud State Normal School,
  67
St. Paul Teachers' Training
  School, 67, 69
School of Organic Education,
  39, 80, 116; opening of, 77;
  role of Comingses in, 77–78,
  79; supported by single-tax
  colony, 78; enrollment in, 78,
  81, 100; northern students
  in, 79, 81, 100–101; supported by Joseph Fels, 79,
  82; as a free school, 79, 100;
  praised and described by
  John Dewey, 80–81, 84–85,
  85–87, 88; as a demonstration school, 89, 106; curriculum of, 91, 92–97, 98–99;
  success of graduates, 97–98,
  110; involvement of students
  with, 99–100; backward children in, 101; teachers in,
  101–3; importance of winter
  course to, 104–5, 108; financial crisis of, 110–13; attitude
  of students toward, 115. *See
  also* Organic education
Sharecropping, 8

Sinclair, Upton: enrolls son
  David in Organic School, 81
Single-tax doctrine, 1, 9; of
  Henry George, ix; as basis
  for Fairhope colony, ix, 5–6;
  and women's rights, 51, 56;
  espoused by Marie Howland,
  59–61; and organic educa-
  tion, 73, 76, 79–80, 105, 106,
  117
Socialism, 51; and cooperative
  colonies, 5; and the Unitary
  Household, 32; and women's
  rights, 59; of Marietta and
  Frank Johnson, 66–67
Social Palace. *See* Godin, Jean-
  Baptiste André
Springfield, Ill.: race riot in, 8
Stedman, Edmund Clarence,
  29, 32–33, 37, 45
Stevens, Ada (Marie Howland's
  sister), 24, 35, 65
Stevens, Melissa (Marie
  Howland's sister), 24, 65
Swift, Alphonso, 68
Swift, Emiline, 68
Sykes, Carrie, 50, 52

*Thirty Years with an Idea* (Marietta Johnson), 113, 133
Topolobampo colony, 21, 22,
  54, 55, 57, 60; plans for, 44–
  45; Marie Howland's life in,
  45–47; interest of E. B. Gaston in, 119
Trask, Sherwood, 102

Unitary Household, 32–33, 34

Village Improvement Club, 51